RHINOS & RASPBERRIES

TOLERANCE TALES FOR THE EARLY GRADES

WITH A FOREWORD BY LOIS LOWRY

ILLUSTRATED BY

LEO ACADIA · NINA FRENKEL · NOAH WOODS

FOREWORD

A note to teachers, from Lois Lowry, about the power of stories ...

THE FIRST STORY I REMEMBER hearing was *The Gingerbread Boy*. I was very young: 3 years old. My sister, new to reading in 1st grade, read it to me laboriously, struggling with each word, and perhaps that's why it is so strong in my memory. Surely my mother, a former kindergarten teacher, had read to me often before. But it is my sister, her forehead wrinkled as she leaned over the book and deciphered the words, whom I picture now in my memory, and whose voice I can almost hear still.

And what, at 3, did I learn from *The Gingerbread Boy*? To talk in rhyme? To run very fast, so I wouldn't be consumed by a cow? Not to be too trusting, so a horse wouldn't eat me? To be cheerful and a good sport when, at the end, I did get eaten by a sly fox?

No. What I learned was that I could be caught up in a story, could become the main character as I listened, could giggle at the funny parts, cringe at the scary ones, could sigh with satisfaction when the story ended, and realize with glee that the book could — and would — be opened again and again.

Stories are the way we rehearse our lives. In the safety of a parent's lap, or the comfort of a favorite chair, the smallest child can experience the fear of the *terrible, dangerous animal* and the relief of the happy ending. Such a story will be told and retold, experienced again and again, and the child will call it forth when her own situation presents a new and scary thing.

Of the stories in *Rhinos & Raspberries*, I especially like the Buddhist tale of Supriya's bowl. It's so simple, so human, so true to our own adult lives. So often we are too busy, too self-absorbed, too lacking in generosity to think of others.

> The Buddha sighed when his eye fell upon the people with hearts of stone. "Is there no one here," he asked finally, "who will take on the job of helping to feed the poor and homeless in these hard times?"

> There was silence. Then a small voice piped up, "I will, Lord Buddha."

The story reminded me of an experience I had many years ago. I was in a small grocery store with my little girl, my first child, who was 4 years old. It was in a city neighborhood, and into the store, as I gathered my groceries from the shelves, lurched a man who was poorly clothed, mumbling to himself, and clearly drunk. I could smell him from where I stood. I took my daughter's hand and moved away from the man, quickly collecting the last few things I needed and moving to the counter so that I could pay and leave. As I stood there waiting while the cashier rang up my items, I could still hear the man talking loudly to himself as he stumbled around the small store, apparently looking for something.

Suddenly I became aware that my little girl was no longer standing beside me. I turned just in time to watch her walk over to the man and look up at him, her big blue eyes looking into his watery, bloodshot ones.

"Do you need help?" I heard her ask him.

The memory of that moment flooded back to me when I read *Supriya's Bowl* and the sentence, *Then a small voice piped up.*

These stories are each of small voices. But what they teach us — and what they will teach small voices yet to be heard from — is very large and very wonderful.

LOIS LOWRY
June 2006 • Cambridge, Massachusetts

Lois Lowry is a two-time Newbery Medal winner — awarded for "the most distinguished contribution to American literature for children" — for The Giver and Number the Stars. She is the author of more than 30 books for children and young adults, including the beloved Anastasia Krupnik series. Publishers Weekly calls her writing "exquisite." Lowry's latest book, Gossamer ($16, Walter Lorraine Books, an imprint of Houghton Mifflin Co., ISBN # 0618685502), a haunting novel that tiptoes between reality and imagination, is available in stores everywhere.

TABLE OF CONTENTS

The Stories

All stories in Rhinos & Raspberries may be read to, with, and by students in grades PreK-6. Discussion questions, writing themes and simple activity ideas are included with each story. More structured, standards-based lessons can be found in the second section of the book.

The Lessons

Standards-based lessons to add dimension to your use of the stories in Rhinos & Raspberries

Character Education & Community Building

These standards-based lesson plans teach tolerance through
Character Education and Community Building. Used individually
or collectively, these lessons can span one day, three days, full weeks
or months — or the entire school year.

Language Arts & Messages of Tolerance

These standards-based lesson plans teach tolerance through
literacy and comprehension. They can be incorporated as part
of standard instruction into most language arts programs.

Student Readers

Two sets of Student Reader books accompany this anthology for use in reading groups and small-group exercises.

INTRODUCTION

For more than a decade, in a feature called Story Corner, Teaching Tolerance magazine has celebrated the transformative power of folktales, fairy tales, fables and parables. This book contains some of our favorite selections from over the years and also offers new stories, written especially for Teaching Tolerance, by noted children's book authors Mary Newell DePalma and Rigoberto González.

Rhinos & Raspberries is for early-grade teachers and their students. Its stories and activities support key educational and social goals. The multicultural tales contained in Rhinos & Raspberries can:

Counteract prejudice formation.

These stories expose and connect students to cultures from around the world. Researchers have studied the effects of such materials on children for more than four decades. As researcher James Banks concluded in the Handbook of Research on Multicultural Education, the use of multicultural materials "can have a positive influence on students' racial attitudes and beliefs."

Improve interpersonal skills.

These stories address a wide range of human emotion and behavior — presenting examples of unkindness and prejudice, as well as examples of kindness and tolerance. The tales will help children empathize with others from various cultures and backgrounds. Research shows that when children develop the ability to empathize, they are more likely to display positive interpersonal skills — something vital in our increasingly diverse world.

Inspire students to stand up against unfairness.

These stories give children a model for active engagement in real-life issues. The inherent message in all of the stories is that children can create more welcoming communities — communities built on kind behavior and respectful language — by working together to understand and diminish the ills of bias and prejudice.

Support culturally responsive teaching.

These stories can help students share cultural knowledge and experience to better understand and more deeply appreciate their own and each other's heritages.

Teachers know that the use of cultural knowledge, prior experiences and performance styles of diverse students increases students' ability to learn.

Bolster literacy.

The lesson plans contained in this book combine explorations of tolerance themes with proven literacy and comprehension strategies. In this way, multiculturalism and traditional language arts programming go hand in hand.

Stories were the world's first curriculum, and they remain a powerful force for change. The stories in Rhinos & Raspberries can help young children envision and create the world in which we all will thrive and grow — together.

JEFF SAPP, ED.D.
Senior Curriculum Specialist/Writer
Teaching Tolerance • June 2006

READING STRATEGIES

Teaching Tolerance encourages teachers to use the following strategies to bolster student engagement with, and comprehension of, the stories of Rhinos & Raspberries — or of any literature:

Before Reading

When students make predictions about a text before reading it, they read with purpose — to find out the answers to their questions and to see if their predictions have come true. Use the following pre-reading strategies with the stories in this book:

VISUAL LITERACY

An artist's rendition adds undeniable power to a story, and visual literacy can aid in comprehension. Before you tell children the title of a story, show them a story illustration and say, "Look at this picture. What do you think the story will be about?" Invite children to share their predictions. Dig deeper with follow-up questions: "What in the picture makes you think that?"

EXPLORING THE TITLE

Now that children have made predictions based on the art, ask them to listen carefully as you read the title. Then ask, "Does the title make you think your earlier predictions were correct? How so?" And follow up with, "Does the title give us any more clues as to what the story will be about?" "Do you see any connections between the picture and the title? What are they?" To keep momentum and interest, add, "Let's read the story now and see if our predictions come true."

During Reading

When reading a story, stop and ask children questions about why characters acted a certain way, what they think might happen next, why things happened as they did, or what they would have done in the same circumstance. Asking students to observe, predict, question, describe and justify hones their interpreting skills and deepens their understanding of the story.

After Reading

Use the discussion questions, activities and lesson plans contained in this book to bolster student understanding of the key elements of a story, such as character, plot, setting, conflict and theme.

READING LEVELS

Reading and grade levels are provided here to aid teachers in using Rhinos & Raspberries for shared and guided reading. The leveling was done based on standardized readability formulas and complexity of vocabulary and concepts.

Raspberries!	Level L, Gr. 2.3
The Clever Boy and the Terrible, Dangerous Animal	Level O, Gr. 3.6
The Prince and the Rhinoceros	Level Q, Gr. 3.9
The Blind Man and the Hunter	Level R, Gr. 4.6
Supriya's Bowl	Level Q, Gr. 4.1
Papalotzin and the Monarchs / Papalotzin y las monarcas	Level Y, Gr. 7.3
Rabbit Foot	Level N, Gr. 3.2
The Fiery Tail	Level U, Gr. 5.5
The Emerald Lizard	Level R, Gr. 4.3
Old Joe and the Carpenter	Level Q, Gr. 4.3
The Stonecutter	Level P, Gr. 3.8
Crocodile and Ghost Bat Have a Hullabaloo	Level X, Gr. 6.6

The Stories

All stories in Rhinos & Raspberries can be used for grades PreK-6.
Discussion questions, writing themes and simple activity
ideas are included with each story.

Student Readers, included with this kit, may be used for reading groups
and small-group exercises, as well as for following along as the teacher reads a story.

Raspberries!
An American Tale of Cooperation

This story is ideal for audience participation, with children speaking along with the repeated sounds.

Three yellow birds lived in a hedge.
Two flew away: **Loop-de-loop! Loop-de-loop!**
The third bird had only one wing and could not fly.
"Tweet-tweet! Tweet-tweet!" she sang sadly.

Pitter-pat! Pitter-pat!
A little dog trotted up to the hedge.
"Why the sad song?" he inquired.

"My brothers are flying
Loop-de-loop! Loop-de-loop!
to the raspberry bush across the street," sighed the little bird,
"and they have left me here all alone."

"We can get there on foot," said the little dog.
So the bird and the dog hip-hop, trip-trotted along the sidewalk.
Pitter-pat! Pitter-pat!
Tweet-tweet! Tweet-tweet!

At the corner, traffic zipped by.
Beep-beep!
Honk-honk!
Zoom-zoom!
WHOOSH!!

"TWEET-TWEET!" cried the little bird, afraid for her life.

"We have to press the button," said the little dog.
"Then the traffic light will turn red, the cars will stop,
and it will be safe to cross the street."

The little bird jumped up and jumped up,
but she couldn't reach the button.
The little dog reared up on his hind legs.
He poked with his paws,
nudged with his nose,
and even swatted with his tail, but he
couldn't reach it, either.

Traffic zipped by.
Beep-beep!
Honk-honk!
Zoom-zoom!
WHOOSH!!

"Chit-chatter! Chit-chatter!"
"What are you two up to?" asked a chatty chipmunk.
"We are trying to cross the street to get some
delicious raspberries," said the bird, "but we can't
reach the walk signal button."

"I'll shimmy on up and press that button!"
the chipmunk said.
She shimmied, but the pole was too smooth, and she
slid and she slid back down.

Traffic zipped by.
Beep-beep!
Honk-honk!
Zoom-zoom!
WHOOSH!!

Along came a frog,
flippity-flop, flippity-flop.
"Whatcha doin'?" asked the frog.
"We want to cross the street,
but we can't reach the walk signal button," explained the little bird.
"Lemme try!" said the frog.
He jumped and he jumped, flapping his floppy feet.
He even tried with his long, long tongue,
but he couldn't reach it, either.

Traffic zipped by.
Beep-beep!
Honk-honk!
Zoom-zoom!
WHOOSH!!

"I have an idea!" chirped the little bird, hip-hopping all around.
"Everyone lie down!"
"Lie down?!" said the dog, the chipmunk and the frog.
"Don't we want to be taller?"

"Exactly!" said the bird.
She stepped onto the frog.
"Hee-hee! That tickles!" giggled the frog.
"Now hop onto the chipmunk," instructed the little bird.

So the frog, with the bird on his back, hopped onto the chipmunk.
"Oooophf! You're heavier than you look!" groaned the chipmunk.
"Now climb onto the dog," said the little bird.

So the chipmunk, with the frog and the bird on her back, climbed onto the dog.
"Ouch!" yipped the dog. "Try not to pull my hair!"
 But the chipmunk hung on to the dog's fur for dear life.
"Now stand up!" said the little bird.

So the dog, with the chipmunk, the frog, and the bird on his back, slooowly stood up.
They balanced like acrobats in a circus.

Swaaay-o!
Wibble-wobble!
The little bird was high,
high up.

Traffic zipped by.
Beep-beep!
Honk-honk!
Zoom-zoom!
WHOOSH!

The little bird pecked
the button, and the light
turned red.
Traffic stopped. It was quiet.
The dog, the chipmunk,
the frog, and the bird
looked this way.
They looked that way.
The walk signal said,
"Walk!" So they did.

Pitter-pat, pitter-pat.
Swaaay-o,
Wibble-wobble!
Tweet! Tweet!

That was quite a sight! But nobody saw them do it. Just at that
moment, the driver coming this way looked down to change
the radio station in his car. The driver going that way consulted
her map. When they reached the other side, the dog slooowly
kneeled down and the bird, the frog, and the chipmunk hopped
off and raced to the raspberry bush:

Tweet-tweet! Tweet-tweet!
Pitter-pat! Pitter-pat!
Chit-chatter! Chit-chatter!
Flippity-flop! Flippity-flop!
Loop-de-loop! Loop-de-loop!

where they ate delicious raspberries all day long.

Mary Newell DePalma wrote
this original tale especially for Teaching
Tolerance's Rhinos & Raspberries.

Illustrated by Leo Arcadia

DISCUSSION QUESTIONS

• Why couldn't Little Bird get to the raspberry bush with her brothers? What did she do to overcome this?

• What did the others do to help Little Bird? Did it work? How did they all work together to cross the street?

• What do you or your friends do to help each other when you can't or don't want to do something by yourself?

• How is working together different from working alone to solve a problem? What are some challenges facing our school or community? How can we work together to help?

DISCUSSION OR WRITING THEMES

Themes that can be explored with this story include:

• **People with differing abilities** (Little Bird's single wing)

• **The value of teamwork** (animals working together to achieve a common goal)

• **The pain of exclusion — and solutions to it** (what it feels like to be left out, when Little Bird's brothers go on without her to the raspberry patch, vs. Little Bird's friends who help her reach the destination together)

• **Solving problems** (the ability to work together, using everyone's strengths, to identify and solve problems or get past hurdles)

FOLLOW-UP ACTIVITY

Grades PreK-3

Dog, Chipmunk and Frog helped Little Bird get across the street to the raspberry bush, where they all enjoyed the berries together. As a class, discuss the ways students have been helped throughout the day or week. ("My brother helped me get dressed this morning," "Someone carried my books for me when my hands were full," "Bobby gave me a pencil when I forgot mine," "Ms. Wilson helped me tie my shoe," etc.) Older students also may draw pictures of someone helping them — a specific person helping in a specific way. Combine the drawings into a "helping" booklet or banner. Or make each drawing into a thank-you card.

Grades 4-6

This story is most suited to younger students; older students, though, can create a project with it by teaching and helping younger students to recite or perform (as a play or puppet show) the story at a school assembly or other gathering. This project could span several weeks and help build bridges between grade levels at your school.

A shorter follow-up possibility for older students is to have them describe (to the whole class or in small groups) a time when classmates, family members or neighbors worked together to solve a problem that couldn't have been solved alone. What was the challenge? How did working together make the task different than if it had been faced alone? Close the lesson by having students write thank-you notes to their helpers.

The Clever Boy and the Terrible, Dangerous Animal

An Afghan Tale of Fear

Once upon a time there was a very clever boy. Nearby was a village that he had never visited. When he was older, he thought he would visit it.

Just outside that village, he came upon a crowd of people who were standing in a field, and as he drew near, he saw that they looked quite frightened. He said, "What is wrong?"

"Oh!" they said. "There is a terrible, dangerous animal in this field, and we are frightened because it might attack us!"

"Where is the terrible, dangerous animal?" asked the boy.

"Oh! Be careful!" they screamed. And the people pointed to the middle of the field.

And when the boy looked where they pointed, he saw a very large melon!

"That's not a terrible, dangerous animal!" laughed the boy.

"Yes, it is!" cried the people. "Keep away! It might bite you!"

The boy said, "I'll go kill this dangerous animal for you."

"No!" they cried. "It's too terrible and dangerous! It might bite you!"

But the boy went right up to the melon and soon was eating a large slice out of it.

The people were astonished. "What a brave boy! He's killed the terrible, dangerous animal!" As they spoke, the boy took another bite out of the large melon. It tasted delicious!

"Look!" they cried. "Now he's eating the terrible, dangerous animal! He is a terrible, dangerous boy!" As the boy walked toward them, the people ran away, saying, "Don't attack us, you terrible, dangerous boy. Keep away!"

And the boy laughed again. "What are you

"What you call a dangerous animal is just a melon," said the boy. "Melons are very nice to eat. We've got lots of them in our village, and everyone eats them."

The people wanted to know how they could get melons, and the boy showed the people how to plant them.

Now they have lots of melons. They sell some, eat some and give some away. They even named their village Melon Village.

And just think. It all happened because a clever boy was not afraid when a lot of people thought something was dangerous just because they had never seen it before.

Adapted from The Clever Boy and the Terrible, Dangerous Animal by Idries Shah ISHK/Hoopoe Books, www.hoopoekids.com, ISBN # 1-883536-18-9).

This story originally appeared in the Fall 2005 issue of Teaching Tolerance magazine.

Illustrated by Noah Woods

DISCUSSION QUESTIONS

• Are people ever afraid of someone they haven't met or someone who is somehow different? Have you ever done that? How?
• How are you like the villagers in this story? How are you like the boy? (As the discussion takes off, use a Venn diagram to capture the similarities and differences.)
• What or who are you scared of simply because you don't know much about them? How can you learn more about them?

DISCUSSION OR WRITING THEMES

Themes that can be explored with this story include:
• **Fear of the unknown or the "other"** (when the townspeople cry out in fear at the sight of something new)
• **The power to make a change** (one person, including one young person, can bring about change, as the clever boy did)
• **Pre-judging** (when the townspeople assume the unknown thing must be terrible and dangerous)
• **Community or helping others** (when the boy helps the townspeople overcome their fears and remains in the community to celebrate the new understanding)

FOLLOW-UP ACTIVITY

Grades PreK-3

Bring in a variety of unusual fruits and vegetables — and melons! — including varieties at least some of the students likely have not tried. Hold one up and ask, "What do you think this is?" If they don't know, ask, "Are you afraid of it?" — bringing the activity back to the story. Then ask, "How can we get to know what it is?" Then ask, "What do you think it tastes like?" Then cut a slice and ask for a volunteer to taste it. Do this with several kinds of fruits or vegetables.

To extend the lesson, have students work in small groups to invent a new fruit or vegetable, drawing and naming it to share with the class.

Grades 4-6

Have students work in small groups to identify a fruit or vegetable they are unfamiliar with. (You may bring a list to get things started, with such things as star fruit, pomegranates, kohlrabi, parsnips, okra, kumquats, gooseberries, scuppernongs, satsumas and so on.) Then have them do research (or provide printed handouts from the Internet) so they can work together to present a report on their fruit or vegetable. At the end of the presentations, bring the activity back to the story by asking, "Now, was anyone afraid of your fruit or vegetable?" Use the lesson to reinforce that fear of differences can be alleviated when we learn about those things we see as "different."

For All Grades

Cap off the lesson with a feast of the now-familiar fruits and vegetables.

The Prince and the Rhinoceros

An Indian Tale of Speaking Kindly

Once upon a time in India, a rare rhinoceros was born, with skin so beautiful it almost glowed. The rhinoceros was given to a noble prince who was very lonely and whose kingdom was poor. The prince was so delighted with the unusual gift that he laughed joyfully. So he named the little calf Great Joy.

The prince treated the rhino with great kindness. He fed her rice, fruit and choice tender plants, and he always spoke in a kind and gentle voice. Great Joy grew and was happy.

The prince thought Great Joy was quite beautiful. At sunrise she would be golden. At sunset, she would be a canvas of pink and red and orange, and later the dark blue of evening. Sometimes after a rain, she would reflect everything around her. She seemed almost enchanted.

"You are wonderful and special to me," the prince whispered softly.

In time, Great Joy grew into an enormous rhino. She was very strong. One day she thought about her good life with the prince and what she could give him in return. "I am only a rhino, but I can use my strength to help him earn gold for his kingdom."

She suggested to the prince that she compete in a contest of strength against the town's strongest bulls.

A rich merchant with many fine oxen agreed to the wager: Great Joy would pull a hundred loaded wagons usually towed by his team of eight oxen. The bet was one thousand gold pieces.

The next day, the prince inspected the wagons and harnessed Great Joy to the front. Then he climbed onto the driver's seat. Great Joy waited for a few kind words of encouragement before starting. Instead, the prince, thinking only of the gold, waved a whip in the air and shouted, "Pull, you big wretch. Move, you worthless rhino."

Great Joy was shocked at her beloved prince's words. Wretch? Worthless? "I'm no wretch," she thought. "I'm not worthless, either." She stiffened her huge legs and refused to move an inch.

Humiliated, the prince ran home and hid in his royal bed. "I'm ruined," he cried.

Great Joy was filled with pain and sorrow. She needed to understand what she had done to deserve such cruel insults. After many days and nights without food or sleep, she went to the prince's palace, which had grown shabby due to his impoverished state. "Oh, Prince, in all our years together, have I ever done anything to hurt you?"

"No, never."

"Then why did you say those terrible things to me? Was the thought of gold worth more than what I can offer?"

The prince hung his head. Tears ran down his face. "The gold distracted me. I forgot the importance of our friendship. I am so ashamed."

"Then we will try again," Great Joy said. "Go back to the merchant and double your bet."

Again the carts were loaded, and Great Joy was harnessed to the front. The prince climbed up and sang out, "All right, you marvelous marvel, you splendid rhino, my Great Joy. It's up to you!"

The powerful rhino snorted, pawed the ground and charged forward. Her sides heaved as she pulled, until the last cart crossed the finish line. The townspeople cheered wildly as they covered her with garlands of flowers and strands of tinkling bells.

The prince collected his two thousand pieces of gold, then humbly thanked Great Joy for a job well done. That very evening, the prince and the rhino walked along the river in the red glow of sunset.

"I didn't mean to say such hurtful words to you," the prince whispered. "Please forgive me."

"I already have," said Great Joy.

And that's how they lived forever after — in friendship and great joy. Never again did an unkind word pass between them.

As told by Toni Knapp in Ordinary Splendors: Tales of Virtues and Wisdoms ($8.85, Roberts Rinehart Publishers, ISBN # 1570980039, out of print).

This story originally appeared in the Fall 1997 issue of Teaching Tolerance magazine.

Illustrated by Nina Frenkel

DISCUSSION QUESTIONS

• What feelings do you think Great Joy had when the prince spoke unkind words to her? Why would the prince have said such mean things to Great Joy?

• When someone speaks mean or unkind words to you, how do you feel? How do you feel when someone speaks kind words to you?

• In the story, how did Great Joy and the prince try again? How can you try again after someone speaks unkindly to you or you speak unkindly to someone? How can you tell that the prince felt sorry about what he had said?

DISCUSSION OR WRITING THEMES

Themes that can be explored with this story include:

• **Kindness and friendship** (the relationship between Great Joy and the prince)

• **Conflict resolution** (how Great Joy handles the unkindness, and how the prince responds to that)

• **Greed or priorities** (when prince thinks of money more than friendship)

• **Apology and forgiveness** (when the prince apologizes for his unkind words and Great Joy says she already has forgiven him)

FOLLOW-UP ACTIVITY

Grades PreK-3

As a class, using a poster-sized piece of paper, list the qualities of a good friend. Make sure to tie specific words — kindness, being nice, not saying mean things — back to the story. Post the list in the classroom as a reminder of being friendly.

Grades 4-6

As a class, discuss this question: "What does it take to be a friend?" Tie answers back to Great Joy and the prince, whenever possible. Then ask, "What happens when a friend says or does something unkind to you?" You may open the discussion with an example of your own, explaining the unkindness and what followed to make amends. Then have students generate a list of three or four "Rules for Kind Behavior" and post them in the classroom. Days or weeks later, if an unkind word is said in the classroom, refer back to the rules and reopen the discussion.

Or, as an alternative activity, frame the discussion around what qualities and actions are used to show appreciation for a friend. Use the ideas to create a "Qualities of Friendship" list, and post it in the classroom as a reminder and discussion prompt throughout the year.

The Blind Man and the Hunter

A West African Tale of Learning From Your Mistakes

Once there was a blind man who lived with his sister in a hut near the forest.

Now, this blind man was very clever. Even though his eyes saw nothing, he seemed to know more about the world than people whose eyes were sharp. He would sit outside his hut and talk to passersby. If there were things they wanted to know, he would tell them, and his answers were always the right ones.

People would shake their heads with amazement: "Blind man, how is it that you are so wise?" And the man would smile and say, "Because I see with my ears."

Well, the blind man's sister fell in love with a hunter, and they were married. When the wedding feast was finished, the hunter came to live with his new wife. But the hunter had no time at all for her brother, the blind man. "What use," he would say, "is a man with no eyes?"

Every day the hunter would go into the forest with his traps and spears. And every evening, when the hunter returned to the village, the blind man would say, "Please, tomorrow, let me come with you, hunting in the forest."

But the hunter would shake his head: "What use is a man with no eyes?"

One evening, the hunter was in a good mood. He had returned home with a fat gazelle. His wife had cooked the meat, and when they'd finished eating, the hunter turned to the blind man and said, "Very well, tomorrow you will come hunting."

So the next morning they set off into the forest, the hunter with his traps and spears leading the blind man by the hand. Suddenly, the blind man stopped: "Shhhh, there is a lion!"

The hunter looked about; he could see nothing.

"There is a lion," said the blind man, "but it's all right; he's fast asleep. He won't hurt us."

They went along the path and there, sure enough, was a great lion fast asleep under a tree. The hunter asked, "How did you know about the lion?"

"Because I see with my ears."

They continued deep into the forest until they came to a

clearing. The hunter set one of his traps and showed the blind man how to set another one. Then the hunter said, "We'll come back tomorrow and see what we've caught."

The next morning they walked into the forest to where the traps had been set. The hunter saw straight away that there was a bird caught in each trap. And he saw that the bird caught in his trap was a little gray one, and the bird in the blind's man trap was a beauty, with feathers of green, crimson and gold.

"We've each caught a bird," he said. "I'll fetch them out of the traps."

And what did he do? He gave the blind man the little gray bird, and he kept the beautiful bird for himself. Then they set off for home.

As they walked, the hunter said, "If you're so clever and see with your ears, then answer me this: Why is there so much anger and hatred in this world?"

And the blind man answered, "Because the world is full of so many people like you — who take what is not theirs."

And the hunter was filled with shame. He took the little bird from the blind man's hand and gave him the beautiful one instead. "I'm sorry," he said.

As they walked, the hunter said, "If you're so clever, then answer me this: Why is there so much love and kindness in this world?"

And the blind man answered, "Because the world is full of so many people like you — who learn by their mistakes."

From that day on, if the hunter heard anyone ask, "Blind man, how is it that you are so wise?" he would put his arm around the blind man's shoulders and say: "Because he sees with his ears … and hears with his heart."

Adapted from Tales of Wisdom & Wonder by Hugh Lupton (Barefoot Books, www.barefoot-books.com, ISBN # 1901223094).

This story originally appeared in the Spring 2000 issue of Teaching Tolerance magazine.

Illustrated by Noah Woods

DISCUSSION QUESTIONS

• What do you think it means to "see with your ears"?

• What did the hunter do that was unfair? What did the hunter do that was kind?

• If you do something wrong and no one sees it, how does it affect you? How might it affect other people?

DISCUSSION OR WRITING THEMES

Themes that can be explored with this story include:

• **Differing abilities** (the hunter focuses on the blind man's "disability" rather than his strengths and abilities)

• **Patience** (the blind man allows the hunter time to learn from his mistakes, without becoming angry or impatient)

• **Pre-judging** (the hunter pre-judges the blind man as weak and without purpose)

• **Apology and forgiveness** (the hunter apologizes, and the blind man forgives)

FOLLOW-UP ACTIVITY, FOR ALL GRADES

Keep a Kindness Chart in the classroom, for a week, a month or all year. Have students report the kind things others have done for them. By adding to the list and watching it grow, children will learn the many ways we can be kind to one another. Pay special attention to kindnesses that involve apologies or people making amends, reminding students of the lesson in this story — that the world is full of people who learn from their mistakes.

Supriya's Bowl

A Buddhist Tale of Giving

Hard times starve people's spirits as well as their bodies. So it was once, when the Buddha lived and famine struck the land. The rains failed, and the heat of the sun withered the harvest in the field. All around, the cries of pain and hunger could be heard.

In the midst of this misery, some people grew greedy and selfish. The Buddha's followers came to him, bringing stories of sadness and shame.

"One merchant in town stabbed another," said one, "and all for a bag of grain."

"I heard of a woman who sold her last goat to buy some flour. On her way home she was attacked by robbers, and the flour was stolen," said another.

"Saddest of all, Lord Buddha," said a third, "are the stories of children dying of hunger on the poor side of town because the wealthy have hoarded all the grain and milk and sugar."

"Call all the people together," said the Buddha.

"Let us see what we can do to help."

So the Buddha's followers called a big meeting. Hundreds of people came. Rich and poor, well fed and starving — out of respect for the Buddha, they came to hear his words.

The Buddha said, "Citizens of this fair land, surely there is enough food in the storehouses of the wealthy to feed everyone. If the rich share what they have in the lean season, then you will all survive to enjoy the benefits of the next good harvest."

The poor and the hungry looked hopeful at the Buddha's words, but the rich people grumbled.

"My granary is empty," lied one.

"The poor are lazy. Let them work for me; then they can use the money to buy the food I have stored," said another.

"There are too many poor people," said a third. "Let them go somewhere else."

The Buddha sighed when his eye fell upon the people with hearts of stone. "Is there no one here," he asked finally, "who will take on the job of helping to feed the poor and homeless in these hard times?"

There was silence. Then a small voice piped up, "I will, Lord Buddha."

Out of the crowd stepped a girl, no more than 6 or 7 years old. She was a merchant's child, dressed in fine silk. Flowers were braided in her hair.

"My name is Supriya," said the child, "and I have a bowl to fill with food for the hungry. When can I begin?"

The Buddha smiled. "Small child," he said, "your heart is filled with love, but how will you do this alone?"

Supriya replied, "Not alone, Lord Buddha, but with your help. I'll take this bowl from house to house and ask for food for the poor. I will not be refused. I know it."

Looking at the child, with her earnest face and shining eyes, even the most selfish among those present grew ashamed.

"I have a little grain in my storehouse," mumbled one.

"I have some pickled mango from summer's harvest," said another.

"My father was poor once. I'm ashamed to have forgotten," muttered a third.

Then Supriya took her bowl, and every day she went from house to house in the rich part of town. Wherever she went, little by little, the bowl got filled.

Sometimes an old grandmother would fill it with rice. Sometimes children would give up their sweets for the day. Often, others would join Supriya with their bowls and help her take the food to the people who needed it.

And sometimes, it is said, when Supriya was tired of walking,

she would rest in the shade of the banyan tree. When she awoke, she would find the bowl had magically filled itself.

"Now," said Supriya, "the hungry will eat, and the people of this town will take care of each other." And so they did.

Adapted from Shower of Gold: Girls and Women in the Stories of India by Uma Krishnaswami (Linnet Books/ The Shoe String Press, ISBN # 0208024840, out of print, www.umakrishnaswami.com).

This story originally appeared in the Spring 2001 issue of Teaching Tolerance magazine.

Illustrated by Nina Frenkel

DISCUSSION QUESTIONS

• What are two reasons that the story tells us that people go hungry?
• Why was it surprising that Supriya was the only one to answer the Buddha's call for help? Was she the richest?
• What could Supriya's bowl represent in our own lives?

DISCUSSION OR WRITING THEMES

Themes that can be explored with this story include:
• **Sharing and charity** (making sure the harvest is shared so no one goes hungry)
• **Selfishness and lying** (those who hoard their food, and those who do not tell the truth when asked to share)
• **The power to make a change** (one person, including one young person, can bring about change, as Supriya did)
• **Community** (those who give to Supriya to make sure no one goes hungry)

FOLLOW-UP ACTIVITY

Grades PreK-3

Create a bowl of good deeds for the classroom. First, brainstorm with children what good deeds might be (saying something nice to someone, cleaning up litter outside, sharing something, standing up for someone who is being bullied, telling another student it's not nice to call names, etc.). List as many as possible, and prompt the discussion as needed ("We've heard a lot about things we can do for people, what about what we say? Can you think of a good deed that involves words?") Once the list is complete, write the items on large slips of paper. Then have children decorate a large bowl together, which will be named the "Bowl of Good Deeds" (or "Supriya's Bowl of Good Deeds," to tie it more directly to the story). Each morning (or once a week, or every month) draw a slip from the bowl and post it in the classroom. Explain that this good deed will be the focus for students for the day/week/month. Afterward, discuss with students what good deeds they performed and how the deeds made them and others feel.

Grades 4-6

Supriya's Bowl is the perfect story to launch a service-learning project for older students. The story specifically addresses hunger, and you can tie it to lessons on world hunger, as well as information about local food banks or soup kitchens that help feed hungry people in your city or town. Students can plan and carry out a canned food drive; they might decide to plant and tend a garden and give the fresh vegetables to a soup kitchen; they might collect pennies and donate them to a food bank or charity. They also can invite other classes to participate, working together to make posters and fliers to advertise the event.

Try to tie the activity to real-world outcomes, letting students know, for example, that their six boxes of food were enough to help feed 10 families for two months. Also, invite someone from the food bank or soup kitchen to speak to the class about working against hunger; or, if possible, organize a field trip to visit a food bank or soup kitchen, where the students can help out directly.

The activity may be tied to written and/or oral reports on the issue of hunger.

Papalotzin and the Monarchs

A Bilingual Tale of Breaking Down Walls

The day finally arrived when the Great North built a Great Wall to separate itself from the Great South. Nothing and no one was allowed to pass anymore, not even the clouds or the wind that once flowed from one side of the sky to the other.

At first, the people of the Great South didn't mind so much. Besides, they thought, they were the fortunate ones: The monarch butterflies had remained on their side of the wall, fluttering around like flakes of orange and gold every day of the year.

But Papalotzin, Royal Butterfly among the Aztecs, was very upset by this. Since time began the butterflies had moved freely back and forth. Their migration was like the circulation of life on Earth!

Papalotzin was right to be concerned. When the butterflies tired of flying in circles before the imposing wall, they began to drop to the ground. Once the monarchs were gone, there was no more color in the sky, and everything began to fade to gray. The sunflowers lost their yellows. The browns of the tree trunks, the reds of the apples, the pinks of people's hands — all of it began to disappear! Even the proud grasshopper became depressed when he was left invisible without his green coat.

The people of the Great South cried for help: "Oh, great Papalotzin, soon we will all be colorless … as death!"

Papalotzin peeked over the Great Wall and discovered that the people of the Great North also were suffering. Everything on the other side also was fading into gray. The strawberries were no longer red. The oranges were no longer orange. And the conversational blue jay stopped talking because he had nothing to say without the brilliant blue of his feathers. "Whatever shall we do?" the people of the Great North cried out.

Papalotzin knew he had to save the people on both sides,

Papalotzin y las monarcas

Un cuento bilingüe acerca de romper barreras

Al fin llegó el día en el que el Gran Norte construyó una Gran Muralla para apartarse del Gran Sur. Nada ni nadie podía pasar de un lado al otro, ni siquiera las nubes, ni el viento que antes había zurcado el cielo.

Al principio, a la gente del Gran Sur no le había importado el asunto. Además, pensaban, eran afortunados. Las mariposas monarcas se habían quedado de su lado. Y allí estaban todas, revoloteando como hojuelas anaranjadas y doradas todos los días del año.

La situación molestó a Papalotzin, dios de los monarcas. Desde tiempos lejanos las mariposas siempre se habían desplazado libremente de un lado al otro. ¡La migración era como la circulación de la vida en la Tierra!

Sus razones tenía Papalotzin por preocuparse. Cuando las mariposas se cansaron de revolotear ante la imponente muralla, empezaron a caer al suelo. Al desaparecer ellas, ya no hubo colores en el cielo. Todo lo demás empezó a descolorarse. Los girasoles perdieron su amarillo. El café de los troncos de árbol, el rojo de las manzanas, el rosado en las manos de la gente—todo ello desaparecía. Hasta el digno saltamontes se deprimió cuando se quedó invisible al perder su abrigo verde.

La gente del Gran Sur ayuda: "¡Oh, Papalotzin!, ¡pronto estaremos tan descoloridos … como la muerte!"

Papalotzin se asomó sobre la Gran Muralla y descubrió que la gente del Gran Norte también sufría. Todo de ese lado también se estaba quedando descolorido. Las fresas ya no eran rojas. Las naranjas ya no estaban anaranjadas. Y el pájaro azul tan platicador dejó de hablar por que ya no tenía más que decir sin el azul brillante de sus plumas. "¿Qué vamos a hacer?" gritó la gente del Gran Norte.

Papalotzin sabía que tenía que rescatar a las gentes de

but also the animals, the flowers, the fruits, and even the sun, which was losing its shine, and even the moon, which was losing its sheen, and even the skies, which were becoming dull as sand.

With his Royal Butterfly foot, Papalotzin kicked and crumbled the Great Wall that divided the Great North from the Great South. He then breathed deeply and blew a gust of wind from his Royal Butterfly lungs to launch the monarchs into the air.

In flight once more, the monarchs spread across the skies; immediately the colors started coming back. Everyone celebrated, North and South: "¡Urraaa! Hooraaay!" The grasshopper jumped in happiness now that he was visible again, and the blue jay sang, joyful in his brilliant blue.

The Great North and the Great South decided it was best to leave things this way, to let the monarchs, and everything and everyone, migrate back and forth for the rest of time. And Papalotzin thought so, too, as he flapped his great wings and pushed the beautiful rainbows high into the sky.

ambos lados, al igual que a los animales, las flores, las frutas, y hasta el sol que ya estaba perdiendo su resplandor, y hasta la luna que iba perdiendo su lustre, y hasta los cielos que se estaban quedando gris como la arena.

Con su gran pié de dios, Papalotzin pateó y derrumbó la Gran Muralla que había dividido al Gran Norte del Gran Sur. Luego resolló profundamente y sopló un aire fuerte con sus pulmones de dios lanzando al aire a las mariposas.

De nuevo en vuelo, los monarcas se desparramaron por todos los cielos y de inmediato los colores regresaron con vida. Todo el Norte y el Sur se puso de fiesta: ¡Urraaa! Hooraaaay! Y hasta el saltamontes brincó de felicidad una vez que volvió a ser visible. El pájaro azul comenzó a cantar, alegre de su color brillante.

El Gran Norte y el Gran Sur decidieron que era mejor dejar las cosas así, que los monarcas, y que todo y todos, pudieran migrar de un lado al otro de así en adelante. Y Papalotzin pensó lo mismo mientras que aleteaba sus grandes alas que empujaban a los bellos arcos iris hacia lo alto del cielo.

Rigoberto González wrote this original tale especially for Teaching Tolerance's Rhinos & Raspberries.

Illustrated by Nina Frenkel

• How do you think the Great North felt about the Great South having all of the glorious monarch butterflies? Why?

• In this story, what happened to everyone when they were sad and trapped by the wall? What happened to them when Papalotzin tore the wall down?

• Why do you think the North built the wall? Were they trying to keep something in, or keep something out?

• Why didn't the North try to rebuild the wall after Papalotzin knocked it down?

• What can we learn from this story?

DISCUSSION OR WRITING THEMES

Themes that can be explored with this story include:

• **Community** (the movement of the butterflies helps create a sense of a larger community)

• **Cliques and ostracism** (when the wall goes up, some are "in" and some are "out")

• **The power to make a change** (someone can remove a wall to rebuild community and reopen lines of communication)

• **Borders and boundaries** (an exploration of the positive and negative aspects of the "walls" we have in our lives)

FOLLOW-UP ACTIVITY

Grades PreK-3

Prior to reading the story — in English and/or Spanish — have students create their own butterflies, in various colors, working from a construction-paper template. Encourage creativity, using glitter, paint and other craft items. Collect the butterflies. Before students arrive on the day you read the story, put all the butterflies in a crowded place, clumped together in one corner of the room. Read the story just prior to lunch or recess, stopping just before Papalotzin kicks down the wall. When the children are out, quickly move the butterflies all around the room, so they are everywhere, not trapped in one place. When the children return, help them notice the changed butterflies, then read the conclusion of the story and work through the discussion questions.

Grades 4-6

To tie this story into your science lessons, study the migration route of monarch butterflies (www.monarchwatch.org is a good place to start) and work together to present reports on the topic. Or tie it to another common springtime classroom activity, the life cycle of caterpillar, cocoon and butterfly.

For the oldest students, this story can serve as a springboard for a discussion or formal debate on current border issues facing the U.S. and Mexico.

Rabbit Foot

An Iroquois Tale of Peacemaking

Many hundreds of years ago, the Five Nations of the Iroquois — Mohawk and Oneida, Onondaga, Cayuga and Seneca — always were at war with one another. They had forgotten their common culture, their similar languages, their lessons to live together in peace. So it was that the Great Creator sent down a messenger to all of the Five Nations. His name was Peacemaker, and he told them many stories about peace and war. This is one of his tales.

Once there was a boy named Rabbit Foot.
He was always looking and listening.
He knew how to talk to the animals,
so the animals would talk to him.

One day, as he walked out in the woods,
he heard the sound of a great struggle
coming from a clearing just over the hill.
So he climbed that hilltop to look down.

What he saw surprised him.
There was a great snake
coiled in a circle.
It had caught a huge frog
and, although the frog struggled,
the snake was slowly swallowing its legs.

Rabbit Foot came closer
and spoke to the frog.
"He has really got you, friend."
The frog looked up at Rabbit Foot.
"Wa'hc! That is so," the frog said.

Rabbit Foot nodded, then said to the frog,
"Do you see the snake's tail there,
just in front of your mouth?
Why not do to him what he's doing to you?"

Then the huge frog reached out
and grabbed the snake's tail.
He began to stuff it into his mouth
as Rabbit Foot watched both of them.

The snake swallowed more of the frog,

the frog swallowed more of the snake,
and the circle got smaller and smaller
until both of them swallowed one last time,
and, just like that, they both were gone.

They had eaten each other,
the Peacemaker said.
And in much the same way,
unless you give up war
and learn to live together in peace,
that also will happen to you.

As told by Joseph Bruchac in On the Wings of Peace
(Clarion Books, www.houghtonmifflinbooks.com/clarion/,
ISBN # 0395726190).

This story originally appeared in the Spring 2002 issue of
Teaching Tolerance magazine.

Illustrated by Noah Woods

DISCUSSION QUESTIONS
• What does it mean to be a "peacemaker"? How do you "make peace"?
• The frog and the snake each wanted to "win." Did either win? Why or why not?
• Who in our classroom or in our school community do you think is like the Peacemaker? Why?

DISCUSSION OR WRITING THEMES
Themes that can be explored with this story include:
• **The dangers of fighting** (frog and snake both end up losing because they keep fighting)
• **Peacemaking** (the Peacemaker advocates giving up war and living in peace)
• **Community** (the opening sequence describes the common ground the Five Nations shared)
• **The power to make a change** (the Peacemaker is able to help others understand the dangers of war and the power of peace)

FOLLOW-UP ACTIVITY
Grades PreK-3
Cut strips of two different colors of construction paper, such as brown and green. The brown strips are snakes; the green strips are frogs. Have children work in pairs to write each other's name (or initials) on a strip, one name on each color of strip. Then explain that the strips represent the snake and the frog in the story, but instead of making each other disappear, they're going to work together to form a strong community. Then set the children up, with a stapler or glue, to create a paper chain, making and linking circles from the slips of paper, alternating between green and brown. Use the chain to decorate the classroom — and to remind children they're connected to a larger community.

Grades 4-6
Do the above activity, but instead of putting names or initials on each slip of paper, write a fill-in-the-blank sentence: Working together, we can _____.

As an extension or alternative, have students work in small groups to draw cartoon sequences or act out scenes of how they can be peacemakers. The cartoons may be posted in school hallways, or the skits may be presented at a schoolwide assembly, spreading the message of peace throughout the school community.

WEB EXCLUSIVE

Download Why Frog and Snake Never Play Together: An African Tale of Prejudice, an original three-act play adapted from folklore by Jeff Sapp.
www.teachingtolerance.org/frogplay

The Fiery Tail
A Chinese Tale of True Beauty

The Peacock Fairy had the head and arms of a woman but had a peacock's tail and body.
All the peacocks in the world wanted to be her apprentice and learn some of her magic tricks.
One day she brought them all together.

"I know you all want to be my apprentice, but I can only choose one of you, and you all look alike,"
she said. "Come back to me at midnight, and don't all look the same!"

They all left making plans to make themselves more beautiful and stand out from the crowd. But one
good-hearted little peacock thought to himself, "I am such an ordinary peacock, there is no hope for me.
I'll just go on my way and not worry about it."

Soon he met an old man who was hot and sweating. Little Peacock gave him some of his tail feathers
to make a fan and cool off.

Then he met a young girl, crying by the roadside. When he
asked what the matter was, she said, "I have been asked to
a dance, and I have nothing good to wear." Without a word,
Little Peacock pulled some feathers from his tail, and gave
them to her, to put in her hair and cover her gown.

And so it went the rest of the day, with Little Peacock
giving away all his plumes to help people in need. Near
dark, he overheard voices from a hut along the road. A
little boy said, "Mommy, I know I must stay in bed to get
better, but I know if I see fireworks at the festival I will be
well. Can't I see the fireworks now?"

"But my child, they don't set off the fireworks until the festival
starts, and it is too early for the festival," answered his mother.

When Little Peacock heard these words, his eyes filled
with tears. "If only I could show him my display of feathers, he might believe they were fireworks." But, sadly, he
had given away all his plumes.

At midnight, all the peacocks assembled before the
Peacock Fairy. Some had fireflies set in their tails to look
like stars, and many had flowers in their plumes. Surely it
would be difficult to choose an apprentice!

"My friends," said the Peacock Fairy, "you all look so beautiful! But I see one who looks very different from the rest. Little Peacock, come here. Where are all your feathers?"

Little Peacock told his story, how he had given away all his feathers to help people. The Peacock Fairy thought for a while, then smiled and said, "Little Peacock, you are the apprentice I want." With a wave of her hand, one plume from every peacock rose in the air and formed a large beautiful fan. Then the fan came down upon Little Peacock's tail!

"Now, I will teach you another trick," the Peacock Fairy said. She whispered magic words in his ear, and, when he repeated them three times, his tail burst into a kaleidoscope of fire!

Little Peacock soared into the air, flying over all the villages with his fiery tail. When the sick little boy saw the fire in the sky, he said, "Mommy, I see the fireworks! I feel better already!" Little Peacock flew through the night, bringing joy and happiness throughout the land.

And so when you see fireworks exploding during festivals, look closely for the Little Peacock with the Fiery Tail.

As told by Hua Long in The Moon Maiden & Other Asian Folktales (China Books, www.chinabooks.com, ISBN # 0835124940).

This story originally appeared in the Fall 1995 issue of Teaching Tolerance magazine.

Illustrated by Nina Frenkel

DISCUSSION QUESTIONS
• What do you think makes someone beautiful?
• Was it how Little Peacock looked or what Little Peacock did that made him beautiful to the Peacock Fairy? Why did the Peacock Fairy choose Little Peacock to be her apprentice?
• What lesson do you think the other peacocks learned from Little Peacock? Do you know someone who is like Little Peacock? How are they alike?
• What could you do today to be like Little Peacock?

DISCUSSION OR WRITING THEMES
Themes that can be explored with this story include:
• **Inner beauty** (it's what's on the inside of Little Peacock, not the outside, that makes him special)
• **Sharing and charity** (Little Peacock gains, rather than loses, by giving away his feathers to those in need)
• **Empathy** (Little Peacock's cries about the ill boy who wants to see fireworks)
• **The power to make a change** (Little Peacock's gifts make a difference in the lives of others)

FOLLOW-UP ACTIVITY, FOR ALL GRADES
Make a bulletin board with a featherless Little Peacock as its center. Explain to the children that each time someone "catches" them being kind or generous, the class will add a peacock feather to Little Peacock's tail. (You may want to set aside a specific time to discuss this each day or each week, depending on how long you extend the activity.) Make paper feathers out of blue, green and purple construction paper. Write the kind deed on the feather and sprinkle some glitter on it to make the peacock's tail shimmer. (Actual blue, green and purple feathers also may be used for decoration.)

As an extension (or as an alternative exercise), have children work in small groups to discuss Little Peacock's behavior and create a scene to act out for the whole class showing how everyone can act more like Little Peacock.

The Emerald Lizard

A Guatemalan Tale of Helping Others

In the 1600s, in the city of Santiago de Guatemala, there lived a priest who had the heart of an angel. His name was Brother Pedro San Joseph de Bethancourt, and the peasants whispered that he could perform miracles.

One hot summer afternoon, Brother Pedro met up with a poor man named Juan on a dusty road. Juan looked extremely worried.

"What troubles you, my friend?" asked the priest.

"It's my wife," replied Juan hurriedly. "She's sick and needs medicine. I have no money. The doctor says she will die without medicine. I don't know what to do."

Brother Pedro wanted to help, but he had no money to give to Juan. Just then, a small green lizard ran across the road. The priest reached down and caught it with a quick grab. Holding the wriggling lizard gently, he placed it next to his heart. The good brother then handed the lizard to the poor man.

Juan was astonished! The lizard had turned into an emerald. He thanked Brother Pedro profusely for his kindness and ran to town. He found a willing merchant and exchanged the gift for medicine, food and three cows. His wife recovered soon after, and Juan knew happiness once again.

Years passed, and Juan prospered in the cattle business. The day arrived when, with a fat purse on his belt, he returned to the marketplace to repurchase the emerald lizard from the merchant.

"I'm sorry," the merchant said, "but the gem isn't for sale. It brings me much luck."

"And so it will today," replied Juan, counting out 10 times the amount he had received for it so many years before.

The merchant grinned. "The lizard is yours, my friend," he said.

Juan searched far and wide for Brother Pedro. At long last he found him living in the countryside.

The old priest, long retired and somewhat infirm, recog-

nized his visitor at once.

"My dear friend," said Brother Pedro. "What brings you out this far?"

"A gift of many years past," answered Juan. "A gift that I now wish to return."

"Come in, come in, and tell me all about it," said the priest. "You are in time to share my midday meal."

Brother Pedro's small house was poor but clean. He offered Juan a simple repast of vegetable stew and dark bread.

Juan told the old priest the story of his prosperity and explained that he wanted to help make life easier for him. He slowly unwrapped the treasure and placed it in the center of the table, next to the loaf of bread. Bright sunlight streamed through the open window, causing the deep-green lizard to shimmer.

Brother Pedro gazed at the marvel for a long moment, then said, "I remember now, and I remember well. It's a thoughtful and loving gesture, Juan. I humbly thank you."

The old priest picked up the gift and tenderly held it to his heart. Then he slowly lowered it to the floor. The lizard awoke and scurried to freedom through the open door.

As told by Pleasant L. DeSpain in The Emerald Lizard: Fifteen Latin American Tales to Tell (August House Publishers, Inc., www.augusthouse.com, ISBN # 0874835526).

This story originally appeared in the Fall 2000 issue of Teaching Tolerance magazine.

Illustrated by Noah Woods

DISCUSSION QUESTIONS

• Why do you think Brother Pedro did not keep the emerald?

• What would you have done with the emerald?

• Besides money or jewels, what are some ways someone can be "rich"?

• How do you think Juan felt when the lizard ran away? Why? How would you have felt?

DISCUSSION OR WRITING THEMES

Themes that can be explored with this story include:

• **Empathy** (Brother Pedro wants to help Juan and his ill wife)

• **The power to make a change** (by giving away the lizard, Brother Pedro is able to change the lives of others)

• **Kindness** (Brother Pedro's actions were selfless, not selfish)

• **Repaying a debt or kindness** (Juan did not forget what Brother Pedro did, and he searched for him in order to repay the kindness)

FOLLOW-UP ACTIVITY

Grades PreK-3

Have students draw something other than money that makes them "rich," using light-colored construction paper they can decorate with glitter and cut into geometric shapes to represent emeralds. (Examples can include family members, friends, happiness, good health, etc.) Then glue these "emeralds" onto darker green paper as background. Post the emeralds around the room.

Grades 4-6

Prior to making the emeralds as described above, have students (as a whole class or in small groups) create a list of the kinds of things, other than money or expensive material goods, that enrich their lives. Then make the emeralds with written messages on them. ("I am rich because my family loves me," "I am rich because Bernard is my friend," "I am rich because people help me when I can't do something," etc.)

As an extension or alternative exercise, have students work in small groups to list character traits of Brother Pedro, then draw a four-panel cartoon showing ways students at your school can behave more like Brother Pedro. Use the Student Reader books to facilitate this small-group exercise.

Old Joe and the Carpenter

An Appalachian Tale of Building Bridges

Old Joe lived way out in the countryside, and he had one good neighbor. They'd been friends all their lives. And now that their spouses were buried and their children raised, all they had left were their farms … and each other.

But for the first time, they'd had an argument. It was over a stray calf that neither one really needed. It seemed as though the calf was found on Joe's neighbor's land and so he claimed it as his own. But Old Joe said, "No, that calf has the same markings as my favorite cow, and I recognize it as being mine."

Well, they were both a bit stubborn, so they just stopped talking to each other. It seemed that a dark cloud had settled over Old Joe … until there came a knock on his door one week later.

He wasn't expecting anybody that morning, and as he opened the door, he saw a young woman who had a box of tools on her shoulder. She had a kind voice and dark, deep eyes, and she said, "I'm a carpenter, and I'm looking for a bit of work. Maybe you'd have some small jobs that I can help with."

Old Joe brought her into the kitchen and sat her down and gave her some stew that he had on the back of the stove. There also was home-cooked bread, fresh churned butter and homemade jam.

While they were eating and talking, Joe decided that he liked this young carpenter, and he said, "I do have a job for you. Look right there through my kitchen window. See that farm over there? That's my neighbor's place. And you see that crick [creek] running right down there between our property lines? That crick, it wasn't there last week. My neighbor did that to spite me. He took his plow up there, and he dug a big old furrow from the upper pond and flooded it.

"Well, I want you to do one better. Since he wants us divided that way, you go out there and build me a fence — a big, tall fence — so I won't even have to see his place anymore!"

And the carpenter said, "Well, if you have the lumber and the nails, I got my tools, and I'll be able to build something that you'll like."

Joe had to go to town to get some supplies, so he hitched up the wagon and showed the carpenter where everything was in the barn. The carpenter carried everything she needed down to the crick and started to work.

The carpenter's work went smooth and fast. She did her measuring and her sawing and her nailing. It was about sunset when old Joe returned, and the carpenter had finished her work. When Old Joe pulled up in that wagon, his eyes opened wide and his mouth fell open: There wasn't a fence there at all.

It was a bridge, going from one side of the crick to the other! It had handrails and all — a fine piece of work — and his neighbor was just starting to cross the bridge with his hand stuck out, and he was saying, "Joe, you're quite a fellow to build this bridge. I'da never been able to do that. I'm so glad we're going to be friends again!"

And Joe, he put his arms around his neighbor and said, "Oh, that calf is yours. I've known it all the time. I just want to be your friend, too."

About that time, the carpenter started putting her tools in the box and then hoisted it onto her shoulder and started to walk away. And Joe said, "Wait, come on back, young carpenter. I want you to stay on. I got lots of projects for you."

The carpenter just smiled and said, "I'd like to stay on, Joe, but you see, I can't. I got more bridges to build."

So she walked on, and there ends my tale.

As told by Pleasant DeSpain in Peace Tales: World Folktales to Talk About by Margaret Read MacDonald (August House Publishers, Inc., www.augusthouse.com, ISBN # 0874837944).

This story originally appeared in the Spring 1998 issue of Teaching Tolerance magazine.

Illustrated by Nina Frenkel

DISCUSSION QUESTIONS

• The story says that Old Joe and his neighbor were "stubborn." What does it mean to be stubborn? Have you ever been stubborn? How?
• How did the carpenter get Old Joe and his neighbor to be friendly again?
• What do you think the carpenter meant when she said she couldn't stay because she had "more bridges to build"? How can we build bridges with each other? Why would we want to build bridges with each other?

DISCUSSION OR WRITING THEMES

Themes that can be explored with this story include:
• **Selfishness** (Old Joe and his neighbor let their selfishness get in the way of their long friendship)
• **Community and helping others** (Old Joe and his neighbor illustrate a damaged community, and the carpenter, by helping out, illustrates rebuilding community)
• **Apology and forgiveness** (Old Joe and his neighbor let go of their grudges and become friends again)
• **The power to make a change** (the carpenter changes Old Joe and his neighbor's life, then plans to go on to change other lives)

FOLLOW-UP ACTIVITY

Grades PreK-3

Remind students of the scene in the story where the carpenter arrives with **"a box of tools on her shoulder."** Then explain that the class, working together, is going to make a toolbox. The "tools" are going to be things people use to make and keep friends. Ask the students, either as a large group or in smaller groups, to brainstorm what those "tools" might be. Prompt as needed with such things as being nice, showing encouragement, helping with math, giving a compliment and so on. Once you have a list, let the students make the tools, working together in small groups. For younger students, you can have pre-made pieces of construction paper in the shape of tools (hammer, saw, wrench, screwdriver, etc.) that students can decorate or label with something from the list. Older students, again in groups, can choose a "tool" to make, then label it from the list. Post the "tools" on the classroom wall, and use them as reminders or discussion prompts if friendliness becomes an issue during the school year.

Grades 4-6

Using the bridge-building images from the story, tell students you're going to build bridges together to create unexpected friendships. Working in small groups, the students will identify two animals from different parts of the world (a zebra and a polar bear, for example) or two characters from separate stories (Little Red Riding Hood and Snow White, for example, or, from this book, Little Peacock and the Clever Boy). Encourage them to be creative; the more seemingly distant the two things, the better. Then have them create a story in which the two become friends. (The zebra buys a lottery ticket and wins a free trip to Alaska, where she meets a polar bear who admires her stripes, for example; or have the Clever Boy be the one who is ill and sees the fireworks at the end, when he shares a slice of melon with Little Peacock.)

Have the groups make drawings or props to tell the story aloud to the class, then post the artwork on the classroom walls.

Afterward, ask students to identify common themes or ideas from the stories. (Someone did something nice for someone else to become a friend; someone stood up for or protected someone else; two characters found out they liked the same food or activity; etc.) Turn this into a "Building Bridges" list that also can be posted in the classroom.

The Stonecutter
A Multicultural Tale of Being Yourself

This circular tale is so widely recorded in Asia, it would be difficult to attribute it to any one region. The magic of the stonecutter changing into anything he wished appeals to children, though even the older ones may need to listen to the story more than once in order to understand how the series of transformations, always from a weaker into a stronger being, ends where it begins.

A stonecutter was chipping away at the face of a mountain.
Clink. Clink. Clink.

The sun was hot, and the stonecutter was tired.

"The life of a stonecutter is hard, and miserable," he said.
"How I wish I was a great and powerful emperor!"

No sooner said than done — the stonecutter found himself transformed into an emperor. He was dressed from head to toe in silks and brocades, riding a carriage of pure gold.

But wait. He was hot inside all those clothes!
The sun was beating down on him.

"So," said the stonecutter, "the life of an emperor is not much better than the life of a stonecutter. I wish, I wish, I wish to be more powerful...
I wish to be the sun!"

In a flash, his wish was granted. He was the great sun in the heavens, the most powerful of all!

But wait. Something was covering him up. Something was more powerful even than the sun. It was a cloud!

"I wish, I wish, I wish to be more powerful... I wish to be a cloud!"

In an instant, his wish was granted. He was a great billowing cloud in the sky, most powerful of all!

But wait. Something was making him move. Something was pushing him

across the sky. Something was even more powerful than the cloud. It was the wind!

"I wish, I wish, I wish to be more powerful... I wish to be the wind!"

And he became the wind. Joyfully he raced across the sky, and swooped down to the earth to bend the trees and stir up the waves in the ocean!

But wait. Wham! Something made him stop. He couldn't move. Something was even more powerful than the wind. It was a mountain.

"I wish, I wish, I wish to be more powerful... I wish to be the mountain!"

And he became the mountain — tall, old, and mighty. Nothing is more powerful than I am, he thought.

But wait.

What was that noise?

It was the hammer of a stonecutter, chipping away at the mountain. The stonecutter was even more powerful than the mountain.

"I wish, I wish, I wish to be more powerful... I wish to be a stonecutter once again."

As told by Judy Sierra and Robert Kaminski in Multicultural Folktales: Stories to Tell Young Children (Oryx Press, Greenwood Publishing Group, Inc., www.greenwood.com, ISBN # 0897746880).

This story originally appeared in the Spring 2003 issue of Teaching Tolerance magazine.

Illustrated by Noah Woods

DISCUSSION QUESTIONS

• The stonecutter was unhappy with who he was and always wanted to change. Are you ever unhappy with something about yourself and want to change it? What is it? Why are you unhappy with it?

• What does it mean to you to be powerful?

• The stonecutter ends up being himself at the end of the story. What do you think this means?

DISCUSSION OR WRITING THEMES

Themes that can be explored with this story include:

• **Equality** (everyone in the story ends up being above and below others, making us all equal)

• **Pre-judging** (each thing the stonecutter identifies as being strong or weak ends up being the opposite as well)

• **The power to make a change** (by changing how you think of things, you can deepen your understanding of them)

• **Self-esteem and inner beauty** (we are powerful and good just as we are)

FOLLOW-UP ACTIVITY, FOR ALL GRADES

Describe stonecutting as a job and open the class for discussion about different jobs that people do. Then go around the class and have each student name a job they'd like to do when they grow up. Pay attention to and highlight choices that break stereotypes ("Lucia wants to be president. Has there ever been a woman president in our country? What about other countries?") or that create common ground among students ("So we have three firefighters in this class. What is it about the job that each of you likes?"). This activity can springboard into inviting someone to speak to the class (a veterinarian, for example, if several students name that profession). If such a visit happens, be sure to ask the speaker what other careers he or she considered, to illustrate for children the variety and diversity of job choices.

Crocodile and Ghost Bat Have a Hullabaloo

An Australian Tale of Name-Calling

In the Dreamtime, all the animal tribes in the outback decided to go on a walkabout. Red Kangaroo, always the most social, had arranged the entire thing.

"It will be a wonderful time for all of us to get to know each other better," Red Kangaroo urged. "We can talk about our families, what we like to eat, where we like to live, and just have a lot of fun."

Red Kangaroo had a very difficult time getting everyone together because some animals liked the night and others liked the day. Finally, they agreed to meet at twilight, the time in between Day and Night.

It started innocently enough. Everyone had been quite nice to each other, getting along well when they stopped for a snack. Koala was chewing eucalyptus leaf salad, and Numbat was quite focused on a termite sandwich. And that's when it happened.

Tasmanian Devil had volunteered to bring a nice stew. When Crocodile asked Ghost Bat to pass the stew, Ghost Bat didn't hear her. Crocodile thought Ghost Bat was ignoring her on purpose, even after Ghost Bat apologized and said he honestly didn't hear her ask for the stew.

"Well I find that a little hard to believe," Crocodile said under her breath, but loud enough for Ghost Bat — with his very large ears — to hear. Others heard, too.

Ghost Bat shot back, "Well at least I don't let my food rot before I eat it." Crocodile was furious. She had long fought against the rumor that crocodiles let their food rot before they eat it, and Ghost Bat knew it simply was not true.

"That's just plain wrong, and you know it!" Crocodile yelled back.

Dibbler Mouse and Wombat took Ghost Bat's side because they, too, had rather large ears. They chimed an old taunt from their childhood aimed at crocodiles: "Rotten food, rotten food, what you gonna feed your brood?"

Then everyone started screaming. Rock-wallaby was called "big foot" by Echidna, and so Rock-wallaby called Echidna a little "puggle." Then Dingo heard someone say something about his dog-breath, and he started howling about how he's not really a dog. So Dingo pushed Emu into a billabong because he thought she'd said it. It went on and on, with everyone calling everyone else names. Red Kangaroo did not know what to do.

And in the twilight of the Dreamtime, both the Day and the Night grew upset.

Looking down from far above, Walu, the sun, was very displeased at the brawl. She hid behind a cloud to keep from seeing the terrible way everyone was behaving.

Then Namarrkun, the lightning man, came out of the sky and made thunder by striking the clouds with the stone axes attached to his elbows and knees. Every time the animal tribes were quarreling, he hissed and crackled until they would stop. He even threw one of his fiery spears to earth to get their attention. That made them scurry into hiding where they'd be left alone to think about the unkind things they'd said to their friends.

And so every time you hear Namarrkun striking the clouds with his stone ax and throwing his fiery spears to the earth, you will know that somewhere someone is name-calling.

Jeff Sapp of Teaching Tolerance wrote this original tale especially for Rhinos & Raspberries, based on Australian culture and mythology.

Illustrated by Nina Frenkel

DISCUSSION QUESTIONS
• Why do you think some people call other people names?
• Walu, the sun, hid behind a cloud during the fight, while Namarrkun made thunder and lightning. Are these the best ways to respond to an argument?
• If you were one of the animals, what would you have done to stop the name-calling?
• Think of a time when someone called you a name. What could you have said so the person would know how you felt? Do you think that would have helped that person learn not to call people names?

DISCUSSION OR WRITING THEMES
Themes that can be explored with this story include:
• **Community** (a large community of diverse animals struggling to work together)
• **Gossip, name-calling and unkind words** (interactions throughout the story)
• **Peacemaking** (intervention to end the quarreling)
• **Cliques and ostracism** (one group judging or arguing with another, identifying its own group as better than another; and stereotypes and how damaging and incorrect they can be)

FOLLOW-UP ACTIVITY, FOR ALL GRADES
Discuss, as a class, the hurtfulness of name-calling. Then ask the students to develop a No Name-Calling contract, something everyone in class can sign — similar to the Declaration of Independence. Post it in the classroom, and refer back to it as needed throughout the year.

For more ideas on addressing name-calling, visit *www.nonamecallingweek.org.*

The Lessons

Use the Student Reader books, included in this kit, to facilitate
small-group activities contained in these lessons.

Speaking Kindly

This lesson is especially relevant to the study of *The Prince and the Rhinoceros* and *Crocodile and Ghost Bat Have a Hullabaloo,* but it may be used with all stories.

Objectives
• Students will learn about speaking kindly
• Students will identify characteristics of speaking kindly

Time and Materials
• One or more class sessions
• Poster and markers to chart student responses

The Lesson
After reading the tale(s), ask the students to define and give examples of unkind speech (name-calling, gossip, bragging, etc.). Gather a sampling of responses, then begin a more focused discussion, asking students to brainstorm specific qualities of a kind speaker. Chart their responses on a large poster and keep it hanging somewhere in the classroom to be used throughout the year. Be sure to guide students to answers that are positive. For example, instead of "Doesn't scream at people," students might say, "Speaks with a gentle voice." Answers will vary but may include the following:

Speaks softly
Speaks gently
Uses "inside voice"
Gives compliments

Uses for the Lesson
When the poster about speaking kindly is on the wall, teachers may use it as a classroom management tool. Reinforce good behavior by walking over to the poster and asking students which quality they are using at that time. The stories become tools for community building in the classroom and the school.

Extending the Lesson
Along with the qualities of a kind speaker, students also can brainstorm the qualities of a good listener. Again, answers may vary — and be aware of, and honor, differing cultural norms. This is an especially good poster to display prominently because listening skills frequently need to be reinforced in the classroom. Examples might include: good listeners nod and agree, pay attention and don't interrupt.

Also, ask students to role-play this activity by breaking into small groups and writing short skits or scenes portraying the negative behavior, followed by a scene showing the positive behavior (or just focus on the positive behaviors, if preferred). Then have groups perform the skits for the whole class. Groups may use the Student Reader books as guides for this exercise.

Developing Character

This lesson is especially relevant to the study of *Raspberries!*, *The Fiery Tail* and *The Emerald Lizard*, but it may be used with all stories.

Objectives
- Students will list and understand positive character traits of the people or animals in the stories
- Students will recognize positive character traits in those around them

Time and Materials
- One or more class sessions
- Poster and markers to chart positive characteristics

These stories feature personal traits that are important for children to develop. For instance, in *The Fiery Tail* children learn that true beauty is not what we wear or how we look, but it is in the way we treat those around us. And in *The Emerald Lizard*, children learn to think of others, not just themselves.

The Lesson
After reading the tale(s), ask students to identify a character and list its positive qualities. Then help them draw parallels between these story characters and their classmates — making sure to avoid the discussion becoming a popularity contest. Offer, or draw from discussion, a few examples:

Character	Positive Quality	Person We Know Who Has This Quality	Other Characters, Other Stories
Little Peacock	Kind	In our class, Wesley because he always smiles and says hello to everyone.	Cinderella, because she never complained.
Little Peacock	Giving	In our class, Clara because she draws pictures for all of us.	The Tree in The Giving Tree, because it gave its life to help the boy.
Brother Pedro	Helpful	In our class, Jailyn because she helps people with their math.	Little Red Riding Hood, because she took food to Grandma.
Juan	Thankful	In our class, Raven because she is always gracious.	The pig who built the brick house, because he didn't get eaten.

Have students break into small groups and ask them to complete this exercise for another character from one of the stories, using the Student Reader books. When everyone is done, share the answers with the class.

Extending the Lesson
A good way to end the school day together involves getting all of the students to sit in a circle and recap the kind things they experienced or observed during the day. Students are recognized for their good character publicly and, consequently, the qualities are reinforced. Example:

Wesley: "Jailyn helped me with my math. That was nice. Thank you, Jailyn."

Jailyn: "You're welcome. I like helping you."

Friendship Without Barriers

This lesson is especially relevant to the study of *Papalotzin and the Monarchs/Papalotzin y las monarcas* and *Old Joe and the Carpenter*, but it may be adapted for use as a friendship theme for any of the stories.

Objectives
• Students will understand what they can do to make friends
• Students will understand the things they do that discourage friendship

Time and Materials
• One or more class sessions
• Poster paper and markers

The Lesson
This lesson examines what it means to be a friend. Many of the stories in this book address friendship. This lesson looks at behaviors that are unkind or unfriendly, compared with behaviors that are kind or friendly.

Discussion
Begin a discussion of the image of the wall in *Papalotzin and the Monarchs/Papalotzin y las monarcas* or the bridge in *Old Joe and the Carpenter*. These questions can guide you:

1. Why do you think the Great North would build a wall around itself or Old Joe would want a fence? Why do you think this? Are there both good reasons and bad reasons?

2. Have you ever seen someone you know "wall out" someone else? What was that like? Have you ever had a friend make an apology — "build a bridge" — after saying or doing something hurtful? What was that like?

3. How do you think it feels to be kept out of something you want to be a part of, or to be put on the other side of a wall or a fence?

4. If someone puts up a wall or fence, what do you think you can do to tear it down? How would you do that?

Extending the Lesson
After the discussion, have students make two lists. The first is a list of what others might say that puts a wall up. An example might be, "You can't play with us anymore." The second is a list of things that others say that tear walls down — or build bridges. An example would be, "We would like it if you played with us at recess today." Keep the two lists up in the classroom and refer back to them as necessary.

As an alternative activity, have students write a letter to a character in one of the stories, describing the ways that character behaves that encourage or discourage friendship.

For more ideas on addressing social boundaries at school, visit *www.mixitup.org*.

LESSON 1.4

Conflict Resolution

This lesson is especially relevant to the study of The Prince and the Rhinoceros, The Blind Man and the Hunter, Crocodile and Ghost Bat have a Hullabaloo and Old Joe and the Carpenter, but it may be used with all stories.

Objectives
- Students will identify conflicts and resolutions in stories
- Students will practice the art of graceful confrontation and reconciliation

Time and Materials
- One or more class sessions
- Poster paper and markers

The Lesson
Students have small and large conflicts during the course of their school day. This lesson gives students specific prompts so that they can confront inequities and injustices gracefully. Students will use the stories to practice confrontation and reconciliation and then make connections to their own lives. Make a large poster of the following prompts and place it in a highly viewed area so that students can refer to it often.

- "I don't like it when you…"
- "I felt sad (or whichever emotion is appropriate) when you…"
- "Please don't do (name behavior) again because it is hurtful to me."
- "I'm sorry that I…"
- "Please forgive me for…"

Example
In pairs, have students choose two characters from any story and, taking on the characters' roles, use the above prompts to confront and reconcile with each other. One student chooses the role of confronter, and the other chooses reconciler.

Ghost Bat: "I felt angry and hurt when you made that comment about my ears, Crocodile. You know I'm quite sensitive about them. Please don't do that, OK?"

Crocodile: "I am so sorry that I lost my patience and said such an unkind thing to you. I should know better, since I've had others make remarks about my long snout. I won't do it again."

Ghost Bat: "Oh, thank you, Crocodile. And I'm sorry for what I said about your food rotting."

Extending the Lesson
Without naming anyone or gossiping and blaming, have students brainstorm a list of common conflicts they experience during a school day (cutting in line, name-calling, not sharing things on the playground, excluding others from activities). Then, using the same format as above, have students pair up and practice graceful confrontation and peaceful reconciliation.

Alternative Endings

This lesson is relevant to all stories in Rhinos & Raspberries.

Objectives
• Students will predict different story endings
• Students will create alternative endings that reflect a tolerance message using any of the stories in this book

Time and Materials
• One or more class sessions
• Chalk board

The Lesson
Many teachers have alternative versions of well-known children's stories in their libraries. Examples include *The True Story of the Three Little Pigs*, by Jon Scieszka and Lane Smith, or *Little Red Riding Hood; A New-Fangled Prairie Tale*, by Lisa Campbell Ernst. These alternative story lines are good examples to invite children to write their own alternative endings to stories in this book. This lesson shows how changing a character's actions or choices also changes the outcome of a story. Positive outcomes, such as reconciliation, are key components in fostering a sense of community.

Example
Using one of the stories, lead students through the following set of questions and record their answers on the board.
• What do you think is the conflict or problem being faced in this story?
• What would be a different way that the character(s) could have faced the conflict or problem in this story?
• If things were different, what are some of the things you think you'd hear the character(s) saying?

Then, with students in small groups using the Student Reader books, choose a different story to examine using these same questions.

Title Only
For PreK-3 students, a title-changing exercise alone can help make the same point. Choose several titles and help the children create different titles that would indicate different endings. Then discuss how the characters' actions might change with the new titles.

Some possible alternative titles to get you started:

Crocodile and Ghost Bat Have a Party

The Clever Boy and the Happy, Friendly Animal

Retelling Stories

This lesson is relevant to all stories in Rhinos & Raspberries.

Objectives
- Students will retell a story in their own words, or through their own drawings
- Retelling will bolster student understanding of the story
- Retelling will increase student understanding of story elements
- Retelling will reinforce student understanding of tolerance messages

Time and Materials
- One or more class sessions
- Retelling the Story handout

The Lesson

Retelling a story is a way for children to show and enhance their comprehension skills. By going beyond showing whether students understood the plot or other story elements, retelling invites children to explain everything in their own words. Retelling helps children internalize the tolerance messages inherent in these stories.

(Most teachers have many graphic organizers for narrative text in their repertoire, such as The Story Puzzle or Project Read's Literature Connection. Many of these graphic organizers work well with this lesson, and teachers are encouraged to use them.)

Simple Retellings

The foundation of retelling is sequencing. To help even the youngest of children, simply ask, "What happened in the beginning of the story?" Next ask, "What happened at the end of the story?" And then go back and ask, "What happened in the middle?" The beginning, middle and end are known as a simple retelling.

Children who have not yet begun to write can be given three sheets of paper and asked to draw each event. Have them number the drawings in order on the back. Shuffle the pictures around and make a game out of putting them in order, each time having the child whose turn it is retell the story. Children use the pictures as cues to retell the story. With each passing turn, the story line gets reinforced. This is also an excellent strategy with second-language learners as it gives them ample opportunity to speak and feel successful as they "read" the pictures.

Older children can be asked to write out the elements of the story and then illustrate them. They also may extend the beginning, middle and end to describe five to seven events, making the story more complex.

Extending the Lesson

An easy way to check student comprehension is to have students turn the story into a news report. Tape a newscast to show students a segment of how an anchor sounds when reporting a story. Next, have students identify key points of the story to use in a newscast:

- Where did the story take place?
- Who are the main characters in the story?

- What are some interesting details?
- Was the conflict resolved? How or how not?
- What will be the first sentence of the story?
- What will be the concluding statement?

To make this fun for students, turn a large box into a make-believe television set and place it on a desk with the student sitting behind it as if they were in the television. This playful activity gets at most of the major components of a story. Make sure that the tolerance message of any given story is included in the news report.

Retelling the Story (PreK-3)   MODEL

A way to teach young students story structure is to use a graphic organizer having them describe the beginning of the story, its middle and its end. Following is an example of a simple retelling for young children. Remember, for pre-school children who don't write yet, you can have them draw the beginning, middle and end. Since this book contains stories of tolerance, have students specifically identify the tolerance message at the end of their retelling. The following is a model.

TITLE: The Prince and the Rhinoceros

BEGINNING
A prince received a gift of a rare rhinoceros and named her Great Joy because she made him so happy. They grew up together, and the prince always said very loving things to her.

MIDDLE
The prince was from a kingdom that was very poor, and one day Great Joy suggested that they hold a contest where they challenge a rich merchant in a contest of strength. Great Joy was sure she could win. But when it was time for the contest, instead of kind words, the prince said mean and cruel words to Great Joy. This shocked Great Joy, and they lost the contest.

END
Great Joy asked why the prince said such mean things to her. The prince apologized, and Great Joy suggested that they repeat the contest. This time, the prince spoke kind words to Great Joy. They won the contest, and the prince never spoke an unkind word to her again.

MESSAGE OF TOLERANCE
The best way to live with each other is to use kind and gentle words.

Retelling the Story

Use these beginning, middle and end boxes to retell the story in your own words. Then decide what you think the main message of the story is, and write that in the "Message of Tolerance" box.

TITLE: _____

BEGINNING

MIDDLE

END

MESSAGE OF TOLERANCE

Retelling the Story (Grades 4-6)

For older students, the beginning, middle and end can be extended by adding boxes. This allows for a more complex retelling. The following example has five boxes, but you may use as many as seven.

TITLE: The Prince and the Rhinoceros

BEGINNING
A prince received a gift of a rare rhinoceros. He named her Great Joy because she brought him so much happiness. They grew up together, and the prince always said very kind words to her.

The prince was from a poor kingdom. One day, Great Joy suggested that they hold a contest where they challenge a rich merchant in a contest of strength. The rich merchant agreed. They would see who could pull a hundred loaded wagons the longest distance. Would it be Great Joy or the town's strongest bulls?

MIDDLE
On the day of the contest, the prince and Great Joy were ready to win. At the moment when Great Joy expected the prince to say something kind to her as an encouragement, he instead said mean things like, "Pull, you big wretch."

Great Joy was so shocked that she didn't even move. They lost the contest and their bet. The prince was crushed, but Great Joy was crushed even more because she didn't understand why the prince would speak so cruelly to her. She moped around for days. Finally, she got the courage to ask the prince if she'd done something wrong. "No," he said. The two talked, and the prince was sad he'd hurt Great Joy.

END
They decided to do the contest over, and they even doubled the bet. This time, instead of mean and cruel words, the prince spoke kindly to Great Joy. They won! And from that day forward, the prince only had kind and loving things to say to Great Joy.

MESSAGE OF TOLERANCE
Kind words give everyone more strength and great joy.

Follow-Up Activities for Retellings
• Have students rewrite a story, but set it in modern times or in the future
• Have students combine two of the stories and introduce characters to each other

Retelling the Story

Use these boxes to retell the story in your own words. Then decide what you think is the main point of this story and write that in the "Message of Tolerance" box.

TITLE: _____

BEGINNING

MIDDLE

END

MESSAGE OF TOLERANCE

LESSON 2.2
Poetry and Tolerance
This lesson is relevant to all stories in *Rhinos & Raspberries*.

Objectives
• Students will retell a story in poetic form
• Retelling will bolster students' understanding of the story
• Retelling will bolster students' understanding of parts of speech (grades 4-6)
• Retelling will bolster students' understanding of tolerance messages

Time and Materials
• One or more class sessions
• Poetry handout

The Lesson
Teachers can use a simple poetry exercise as a way to retell these stories of tolerance. While emphasizing the core tolerance message, these poetry structures also increase comprehension and literacy skills. The following are provided as examples.

PARTS OF SPEECH POETRY PATTERN	EXAMPLE from *The Fiery Tail*
Title	Petite Peacock
Adjective, adjective noun	Glistening, fiery tail
Verb adverb (-ly)	Giving selflessly*
Adjective noun, adjective noun	Feathery gifts, smiling faces
Noun verb adverb (-ly)	Fireworks exploding brightly

Story Triangle Pattern
(This format works well for younger students who don't yet know the parts of speech, or as a group exercise, led by the teacher, with the class creating a poem together.)

STORY TRIANGLE PATTERN	EXAMPLE from *The Fiery Tail*
Main character	Little Peacock
Two words to describe the setting	Country road
Three words to describe the character	He helps others*
Four-word sentence describing an event	Peacock Fairy chooses him
Five-word sentence describing another event	He brightens the boy's life*

Be certain to emphasize including the message of tolerance in each poem.

Poetry and Tolerance

PARTS OF SPEECH POETRY PATTERN

Title
Adjective, adjective noun
Verb adverb (-ly)
Adjective noun, adjective noun
Noun verb adverb (-ly)

EXAMPLE from *The Fiery Tail*

Petite Peacock
Glistening, fiery tail
Giving selflessly
Feathery gifts, smiling faces
Fireworks exploding brightly

Choose a story and write your own parts of speech poem

_____

_____

_____

_____

_____

STORY TRIANGLE PATTERN

Main character
Two words to describe the setting
Three words to describe the character
Four-word sentence describing an event
Five-word sentence describing another event

EXAMPLE from *The Fiery Tail*

Little Peacock
Country road
He helps others
Peacock Fairy chooses him
He brightens the boy's life

Choose a story and write your own story triangle

_____

_____

_____

_____

_____

Story Structure and Tolerance

This lesson is relevant to all stories in *Rhinos & Raspberries*.

Objectives
• Students will understand the tolerance message of a particular story
• Students will identify the tolerance message through exploration of main character, setting and plot

Time and Materials
• One or more class sessions
• Story Structure handout

The Lesson
Use this lesson to reinforce the tolerance message in each of the stories. All stories contain basic elements. For example, all stories have a time frame, a main character, supporting characters, setting, conflict/problem, events and an ending. Together, these elements make up the story structure.

Elements to be discussed in this lesson are character, setting, plot and theme (or message). To begin, take one of the stories and do a "think aloud" with students.

The Process
After the story has been read, work through the following as a class, recording each element on the board:

• "The main character of a story is the person or animal that you think is most important (or has the biggest wish in the story). You must tell why you think that character is most important (or what the character's wish is and what is standing in the way of that wish coming true). In this story, I think _____ is the main character because _____."

• "The setting of the story is where it takes place. The story tells me that it took place in/at _____."

• All good stories have a conflict or problem that is somehow resolved. "The conflict or problem in this story is _____ _____."

• "The plot of a story is the series of events that happens in the story. The plot of this story is _____."

• "The theme or message of the story is the main point the story is trying to get across to the reader. I think the main point, or tolerance message, of this story is _____ because _____."

Small Group Practice
Working in small groups and using the Student Reader books, students select a tale and repeat this process to identify the main character, setting, conflict/problem, plot and tolerance message. Make it clear that the emphasis is on a supportive conversation rather than finding a right answer; students may disagree about who the main character is or what the message is, for example. The process will help students learn there are different ways to interpret stories. Have students report to the class what they have found regarding the key literary elements.

Independent Work

Now that the teacher has modeled the task and the students have had practice in small groups, it is time for students to do this independently. Students may use the "Story Structure" handout as a guide for an independent exploration of the key literary elements.

For Younger Students

Focus on character and message with younger students, asking them to draw the main character and explain what that character learned in the story.

Other Ways to Discuss Story Structure

• Name other characters in the story. List a characteristic about each one.
• Describe some things that happened as the characters tried to solve the problem in the story.
• Talk about how the story ended.
• Talk about whether you liked or didn't like the story. Give reasons for your opinion.
• What is the main message of the story? How does that apply to your own life?

Story Structure

TITLE OF STORY: _____

The **main character** of this tale is …
Describe the main character:_____

_____

_____

_____

The **setting** of this tale is …
Describe the setting in as much detail as possible:_____

_____

_____

_____

The **plot** is about the events that take place in the story. This story's events are …

1. _____

2. _____

3. _____

4. _____

5. _____

The **message** of this story is …

_____

_____

_____

_____

Writing Your Own Tales Of Tolerance

This lesson is relevant to all stories in *Rhinos & Raspberries*.

Objectives
• Students will write their own version of one of the stories in this book
• Students will illustrate the story

Time and Materials
• Three class sessions (to draft, edit and rewrite the story)

The Lesson

A simple way to lead children to success in story writing is to have them use a familiar story as a model, changing only a few elements for them to write their own versions based on their own environments.

So, *The Emerald Lizard* becomes *The Ruby Snake*. Or the animals represented in *Crocodile and Ghost Bat Have a Hullabaloo* can be switched to represent animals from the students' own geographic environment. Or *The Fiery Tail* can become *The Colorful Hat*.

The only thing that really changes in students' retelling of one of these tales is the setting and the characters. The plot, story line and events remain basically the same. Also have children illustrate their story.

For younger children, a picture version of the story accomplishes the same goal, or, more simply, a drawing of a character in its original form and in its new form.

What Would You Do?

This lesson is relevant to all stories in *Rhinos & Raspberries*.

Objectives
• Students will write their own version of a story from this book, casting themselves in a main role
• Students will illustrate the story
• Students will understand the ability a person has to make choices and change outcomes

Time and Materials
• Three class sessions (to draft, edit and rewrite the story)

The Lesson
Building on Lesson 2.4, or done individually, this lesson asks students to cast themselves in key roles in the stories, making their own decisions when faced with similar challenges. In the new version, each student will write and illustrate one of the tales, taking on the role of one of the characters. By personalizing a story, students will realize the power they have to make choices — and learn that such choices have consequences. In the end, children can read or act out their stories for the class.

For younger children, a picture version of the story accomplishes the same goal, or, more simply, a drawing of a character in its original form and a second drawing of a student in that role. Using the drawings, children can discuss what they would do differently as each character, and how that might change the ending of the story.

This lesson also builds on the reading strategy described in the introduction, a logical extension of asking, during the reading of stories, "What would you do in that situation?" or, "What choice would you make?"

Follow-Up Activity
Once the stories have been shared, have students choose another student's new character and write a letter to the student, describing what changes were noticed and praising the student for wise or kind choices he or she made. Children can share these letters in small groups.

Standards

The content provided in this book supports the goals and objectives of your state content standards. The lessons may be used to address the academic standards listed below. The standards are drawn from *Content Knowledge: A Compendium of Standards and Benchmarks for K-12 Education*, 4th Edition (www.mcrel.org/standards-benchmarks).

Language Arts Standards

Standard Uses the general skills and strategies of the writing process

Benchmark Pre-K Knows that writing, including pictures, letters and words, communicates meaning and information

Benchmark Pre-K Uses drawings to express thoughts, feelings and ideas

Benchmark Pre-K Uses emergent writing skills to write for a variety of purposes (e.g., to make lists, to send messages, to write stories) and to write in a variety of forms (e.g., journals, sign-in sheets, name cards, cards with words and pictures)

Benchmark Pre-K Uses knowledge of letters to write or copy familiar words, such as own name

Benchmark Pre-K Uses writing tools and materials (e.g., pencils, crayons, chalk, markers, rubber stamps, computers, paper, cardboard, chalkboard)

Benchmark K-2 Prewriting: Uses prewriting strategies to plan written work (e.g., discusses ideas with peers, draws pictures to generate ideas, writes key thoughts and questions, rehearses ideas, records reactions and observations)

Benchmark K-2 Drafting and Revising: Uses strategies to draft and revise written work (e.g., rereads; rearranges words, sentences and paragraphs to improve or clarify meaning; varies sentence type; adds descriptive words and details; deletes extraneous information; incorporates suggestions from peers and teachers; sharpens the focus)

Benchmark K-2 Editing and Publishing: Uses strategies to edit and publish written work (e.g., proofreads using a dictionary and other resources; edits for grammar, punctuation, capitalization and spelling at a developmentally appropriate level; incorporates illustrations or photos; uses available, appropriate technology to compose and publish work; shares finished product)

Benchmark K-2 Evaluates own and others' writing (e.g., asks questions and makes comments about writing, helps classmates apply grammatical and mechanical conventions)

Benchmark K-2 Uses strategies to organize written work (e.g., includes a beginning, middle and ending; uses a sequence of events)

Benchmark 3-6 Prewriting: Uses prewriting strategies to plan written work (e.g., uses graphic organizers, story maps and webs; groups related ideas; takes notes; brainstorms ideas; organizes information according to type and purpose of writing)

Benchmark 3-6 Drafting and Revising: Uses strategies to draft and revise written work (e.g., elaborates on a central idea; writes with attention to audience, word choice, sentence variation; uses paragraphs to develop separate ideas; produces multiple drafts)

Benchmark 3-6 Editing and Publishing: Uses strategies to edit and publish written work (e.g., edits for grammar, punctuation, capitalization and spelling at a developmentally appropriate level; uses reference materials; considers page format [paragraphs, margins, indentations, titles]; selects presentation format according to purpose; incorporates photos, illustrations, charts and graphs; uses available technology to compose and publish work)

Benchmark 3-6 Evaluates own and others' writing (e.g., determines the best features of a piece of writing, determines how own writing achieves its purposes, asks for feedback, responds to classmates' writing)

Benchmark 3-6 Uses strategies (e.g., adapts focus, organization, point of view; determines knowledge and interests of audience) to write for different audiences (e.g., self, peers, teachers, adults)

Benchmark 3-6 Uses strategies (e.g., adapts focus, point of view, organization, form) to write for a variety of purposes (e.g., to inform, entertain, explain, describe, record ideas)

Benchmark 3-6 Writes expository compositions (e.g., identifies and stays on the topic; develops the topic with simple facts, details, examples and explanations; excludes extraneous and inappropriate information; uses structures such as cause-and-effect, chronology, similarities and differences; uses several sources of information; provides a concluding statement)

Benchmark 3-6 Writes narrative accounts, such as poems and stories (e.g., establishes a context that enables the reader to imagine the event or experience; develops characters, setting and plot; creates an organizing structure; sequences events; uses concrete sensory details; uses strategies such as dialogue, tension and suspense; uses an identifiable voice)

Benchmark 3-6 Writes expressive compositions (e.g., expresses ideas, reflections and observations; uses an individual, authentic voice; uses narrative strategies, relevant details and ideas that enable the reader to imagine the world of the event or experience)

Benchmark 3-6 Writes in response to literature (e.g., summarizes main ideas and significant details; relates own ideas to supporting details; advances judgments; supports judgments with references to the text, other works, other authors, nonprint media and personal knowledge)

Art Connections

Standard Understands connections among the various art forms and other disciplines

Benchmark K-4 Knows how ideas (e.g., sibling rivalry, respect) and emotions (e.g., sadness, anger) are expressed in the various art forms

Visual Arts

Standard Understands and applies media, techniques and processes related to the visual arts

Benchmark Pre-K Experiments with a variety of colors, textures and shapes

Benchmark Pre-K Uses a variety of basic art materials (e.g., paints, crayons, clay, pencils) to create works of art and express ideas and feelings

Benchmark Pre-K Knows the names of a few of the basic colors

Benchmark K-4 Knows how different materials, techniques and processes cause different responses from the viewer

Benchmark K-4 Knows how different media (e.g., oil, watercolor, stone, metal), techniques and processes are used to communicate ideas, experiences and stories

Benchmark K-4 Uses art materials and tools in a safe and responsible manner

Benchmark 5-6 Understands what makes different art media, techniques and processes effective (or ineffective) in communicating various ideas

Benchmark 5-6 Knows how the qualities and characteristics of art media, techniques and processes can be used to

enhance communication of experiences and ideas

Standard Knows how to use structures (e.g., sensory qualities, organizational principles, expressive features) and functions of art

Benchmark K-4 Knows the differences among visual characteristics (e.g., color, texture) and purposes of art (e.g., to convey ideas)

Benchmark K-4 Understands how different compositional, expressive features (e.g., evoking joy, sadness, anger), and organizational principles (e.g., repetition, balance, emphasis, contrast, unity) cause different responses

Benchmark K-4 Uses visual structures and functions of art to communicate ideas

Benchmark 5-6 Knows how the qualities of structures and functions of art are used to improve communication of one's ideas

Standard Knows a range of subject matter, symbols and potential ideas in the visual arts

Benchmark K-4 Selects prospective ideas (e.g., formulated thoughts, opinions, concepts) for works of art

Benchmark K-4 Knows how subject matter, symbols and ideas are used to communicate meaning

Benchmark 5-6 Knows different subjects, themes and symbols (through context, value and aesthetics) that convey intended meaning in artworks

Standard Understands the characteristics and merits of one's own artwork and the artwork of others

Benchmark Pre-K Discusses and evaluates the intentions and meanings of his or her own artwork and the work of others

Benchmark K-4 Understands that specific artworks can elicit different responses

Benchmark 5-6 Understands how one's own artworks, as well as artworks from various eras and cultures, may elicit a variety of responses

Character Education

Character qualities mentioned in this handbook (citizenship, compassion, respect, etc.) are taken from *The Center for Advancement of Ethics and Character* at Boston University. Its *Character Education Manifesto* states, "Character education is not merely a trend or the school's latest fad; character education is a fundamental dimension of good teaching." *www.bu.edu/education/caec/*

Recommended Resources

Action Strategies for Deepening Comprehension
Jeffrey D. Wilhelm, Ph.D.
Scholastic Publishers
ISBN # 0-439-21857-8
$19.95
(800) SCHOLASTIC
http://teacher.scholastic.com/products/
product_info/

Boys and Girls: Superheroes in the Doll Corner
Vivian Gussin Paley
University of Chicago Press
ISBN # 0226644928
$12.00
(773) 702-7700
www.press.uchicago.edu

Fair is Fair: World Folktales of Justice
Sharon Creeden
August House Publishers
ISBN # 0-87483-477-5
$12.95
(800) 284-8784
www.augusthouse.com

Fearless Girls, Wise Women & Beloved
Sisters: Heroines in Folktales from
Around the World
Kathleen Ragan
W. W. Norton & Company
ISBN # 0-393-32046-4
$16.95
800-233-4830
www.wwnorton.com/orders

Happily Ever After: Sharing Folk Literature
With Elementary and Middle School Students
Terrell A. Young
International Reading Association
ISBN # 0-87207-510-9
$34.95
(800) 336-7323 ext 266
www.reading.org/publications/bbv/books/bk510/

Inside Picture Books
Ellen Handler Spitz
Yale University Press
ISBN: 0300084765
$13.95
(800) 405-1619
http://yalepress.yale.edu/yupbooks

Killing Monsters: Our Children's Need
for Fantasy, Heroism and Make-Believe
Violence
Gerard Jones
Basic Books
ISBN # 0465036961
$15.00
(800) 343-4499
www.basicbooks.com

Primary Story Puzzle
Victoria Greene and
Mary Lee Enfield, Ph.D.
Project Read, Language Circle®
Enterprises, Inc.
Item # 26081
$25.00
(800) 450-0343
www.projectread.com/uploads/
LC05-06Catalog.pdf

Storyteller, Storyteacher: Discovering the
Power of Storytelling for Teaching
and Living
Marni Gillard
Stenhouse Publishers
ISBN # 1-57110-014-8
$19.50
(800) 988-9812
www.stenhouse.com

Teaching as Story Telling
Kieran Egan
University of Chicago Press
ISBN # 0-226-19032-3

$12.00
(773) 702-7700
www.press.uchicago.edu

Teaching Reading Through
Balanced Literacy
Jeff Sapp
Phi Delta Kappa International
Item# HTTRBL
$30.00
(800) 766-1156
www.pdkintl.org

Touch Magic
Jane Yolen
August House Publishers
ISBN # 0-87483-591-7
$11.95
(800) 284-8784
www.augusthouse.com

WEBSITES

Teaching Tolerance reviews a variety
of multicultural resources.
www.tolerance.org/teach/magazine

The Anti-Defamation League World of
Difference recommends multicultural
and anti-bias books for children.
www.adl.org/bibliography/

Reading A-Z is a membership website
that has about 1,600 downloadable
books, including folktales from around
the world with themes of tolerance
and character education. There are 30
free samples.
www.Readinga-z.com

Credits & Acknowledgments

Stories selected by: Jeff Sapp
Lesson plans and activities by: Jeff Sapp

Project Manager: Brian Willoughby
Consulting Editor: Jennifer Holladay

Reviewers: Pamela Abrams, New York-based editor, writer, parenting expert and author; Temisha L. El-liott, Montessori at Greenwood Plaza, Denver, Colo.; Connie Ramsey, Colbert Elementary School, Mead (Wash.) School District, National Board Certified teacher in the area of literacy; Connie Rockman, children's literature consultant, Stratford, Conn.

Literacy consultant: Kimberly Skach

Staff Editors: Annie Bolling, Lecia J. Brooks, J. Richard Cohen, Carrie Kilman, Colleen O'Brien, Rhonda Thomason

Design Director: Russell Estes
Senior Designer: Valerie Downes
Designer: Crystal Phillips
Print Production: Betty Ruff
Web Production: Ryan King
Rights Coordinator: Rosi Smith

With special thanks to the authors who contributed original works to Rhinos & Raspberries, and to the publishers and authors who allowed us to reprint their stories ...

THE CLEVER BOY AND THE TERRIBLE, DANGEROUS ANIMAL Adapted from *The Clever Boy and the Terrible, Dangerous Animal* by Idries Shah ISHK/Hoopoe Books, www.hoopoekids.com, ISBN # 1-883536-18-9). This story originally appeared in the Fall 2005 issue of *Teaching Tolerance* magazine. The use of *The Clever Boy and the Terrible, Dangerous Animal* by Idries Shah is by permission from the publisher, ISHK/Hoopoe Books, www.hoopoebooks.com.

THE PRINCE AND THE RHINOCEROS As told by Toni Knapp in *Ordinary Splendors: Tales of Virtues and Wisdoms* ($8.85, Roberts Rinehart Publishers, ISBN # 1570980039, out of print). This story originally appeared in the Fall 1997 issue of *Teaching Tolerance* magazine. ©1995 by Toni Knapp. Reprinted by permission from *Ordinary Splendors: Tales of Virtues and Wisdoms* (Roberts Rinehart Publishers).

THE BLIND MAN AND THE HUNTER Adapted from *Tales of Wisdom & Wonder* by Hugh Lupton (Barefoot Books, www.barefoot-books.com, ISBN # 1901223094). This story originally appeared in the Spring 2000 issue of *Teaching Tolerance* magazine. ©1998 by Hugh Lupton. Adapted from *Tales of Wisdom & Wonder* and reprinted by permission of Barefoot Books.

SUPRIYA'S BOWL Adapted from *Shower of Gold: Girls and Women in the Stories of India* by Uma Krishnaswami (Linnet Books/The Shoe String Press, ISBN # 0208024840, out of print, www.umakrishnaswami.com). This story originally appeared in the Spring 2001 issue of *Teaching Tolerance* magazine. ©1999 by Uma Krishnaswami. Adapted from *Shower of Gold: Girls and Women in the Stories of India* (Linnet Books/The Shoe String Press)

RABBIT FOOT As told by Joseph Bruchac in *On the Wings of Peace* (Clarion Books, www.houghtonmifflinbooks.com/clarion/, ISBN # 0395726190). This story originally appeared in the Spring 2002 issue of *Teaching Tolerance* magazine. ©1995 by Joseph Bruchac. Reprinted by permission of Joseph Bruchac from *On the Wings of Peace* (Clarion Books).

THE FIERY TAIL As told by Hua Long in *The Moon Maiden & Other Asian Folktales* (China Books, www.chinabooks.com, ISBN # 0835124940). This story originally appeared in the Fall 1995 issue of *Teaching Tolerance* magazine. ©1995 by Hua Long. Reprinted by permission from *The Moon Maiden & Other Asian Folktales* (China Books).

THE EMERALD LIZARD As told by Pleasant L. DeSpain in *The Emerald Lizard: Fifteen Latin American Tales to Tell* (August House Publishers, Inc., www.augusthouse.com, ISBN # 0874835526). This story originally appeared in the Fall 2000 issue of *Teaching Tolerance* magazine. ©1999 by Pleasant L. DeSpain. Reprinted by permission from *The Emerald Lizard: Fifteen Latin American Tales to Tell* (August House Publishers, Inc.).

OLD JOE AND THE CARPENTER As told by Pleasant DeSpain in *Peace Tales: World Folktales to Talk About* by Margaret Read MacDonald (August House Publishers, Inc., www.augusthouse.com, ISBN # 0874837944). This story originally appeared in the Spring 1998 issue of *Teaching Tolerance* magazine. ©1992 by Pleasant L. DeSpain. Reprinted by permission from *Peace Tales: World Folktales to Talk About* by Margaret Read MacDonald (August House Publishers, Inc.).

THE STONECUTTER As told by Judy Sierra and Robert Kaminski in *Multicultural Folktales: Stories to Tell Young Children* (Oryx Press, Greenwood Publishing Group, Inc., www.greenwood.com, ISBN # 0897746880). This story originally appeared in the Spring 2003 issue of *Teaching Tolerance* magazine. ©1991 by Judy Sierra and Robert Kaminski. Reprinted by permission from *Multicultural Folktales: Stories to Tell Young Children* (Greenwood Publishing Group. Inc., Westport, CT).

PAPALOTZIN AND THE MONARCHS Rigoberto González wrote this original tale especially for Teaching Tolerance's *Rhinos & Raspberries*. He is the author of *Antonio's Card/La tarjeta de Antonio* (Children's Book Press, $16.95, ISBN # 0-89239-204-5) and *Soledad Sigh-Sighs/Soledad suspiros*. Born in Bakersfield, Calif., and raised in Michoacán, Mexico, González is the son and grandson of migrant farm workers. Visit www.rigobertogonzalez.com.

CROCODILE AND GHOST BAT HAVE A HULLABALOO Jeff Sapp of Teaching Tolerance wrote this original tale especially for *Rhinos & Raspberries*, based on Australian culture and mythology. Sapp is a senior curriculum specialist and writer with Teaching Tolerance. A former classroom teacher, Sapp received his doctorate in education in 1993 from West Virginia University. He speaks internationally on children's literature and brain-compatible learning and has published in numerous peer-reviewed journals, including *Multicultural Education* and *Encounter: Education for Meaning and Social Justice*. In 2002, Phi Delta Kappa International published his first book, *Teaching Reading Through Balanced Literature*. Visit www.jeffsapp.com.

And to the illustrators who contributed to Rhinos & Raspberries ...
Nina Frenkel lives in Brooklyn, where she illustrates and animates for a living. She is a big fan of learning and teaches Animation Design to young students at the Parsons School of Design in New York City. You can see her work at www.ninafrenkel.com.

Noah Woods is a Los Angeles native and graduate of UCLA and Art Center College of Design. His children's book *Tom Cat* (published by Random House) was named one of the ten best picture books of 2004 by Disney and Scholastic. Noah is presently on faculty at Art Center College of Design.

Leo Acadia is a fake!... Actually, John S. Dykes markets his digital creations under the name Leo Acadia (the styles are very different). Leo has been recognized with awards from The Society of Illustrators, Communication Arts, and American Illustration. They both work out of the same studio in Sudbury, Massachusetts., but are rarely seen in the same place at the same time...Hmmmmm. Visit www.leoacadia.com and www.jsdykes.com.

And, finally, thanks to the supporters of the Southern Poverty Law Center whose generosity made this project possible.